12 7-17

...tablished
...el brands,
...in travel.

For more than 135 years our
guidebooks have unlocked the secrets
of destinations around the world,
sharing with travellers a wealth of
experience and a passion for travel.

**Rely on Thomas Cook as your
travelling companion on your next trip
and benefit from our unique heritage.**

Thomas Cook **pocket** guides

MALTA
Paul Murphy

Written by Paul Murphy, updated by Richard Williams

Published by Thomas Cook Publishing
A division of Thomas Cook Tour Operations Limited
Company Registration no. 3772199 England
The Thomas Cook Business Park, Unit 9, Coningsby Road,
Peterborough PE3 8SB, United Kingdom
Email: books@thomascook.com, Tel: +44 (0) 1733 416477
www.thomascookpublishing.com

Produced by Cambridge Publishing Management Limited
Burr Elm Court, Main Street, Caldecote CB23 7NU
www.cambridgepm.co.uk

ISBN: 978-1-84848-535-8

© 2006, 2008, 2010 Thomas Cook Publishing
This fourth edition © 2011
Text © Thomas Cook Publishing
Maps © Thomas Cook Publishing/PCGraphics (UK) Limited

Series Editor: Karen Beaulah
Production/DTP Editor: Steven Collins

Printed and bound in Spain by GraphyCems

Cover photography © Charles O. Cecil/Alamy

CONTENTS

WHAT'S IN YOUR GUIDEBOOK?

Independent authors Impartial, up-to-date information from our travel experts who meticulously source local knowledge.

Experience Thomas Cook's 165 years in the travel industry and guidebook publishing enriches every word with expertise you can trust.

Travel know-how Thomas Cook has thousands of staff working around the globe, all living and breathing travel.

Editors Travel-publishing professionals, pulling everything together to craft a perfect blend of words, pictures, maps and design.

You, the traveller We deliver a practical, no-nonsense approach to information, geared to how you really use it.

● *Valletta's waterfront*

INTRODUCTION
Getting to know Malta

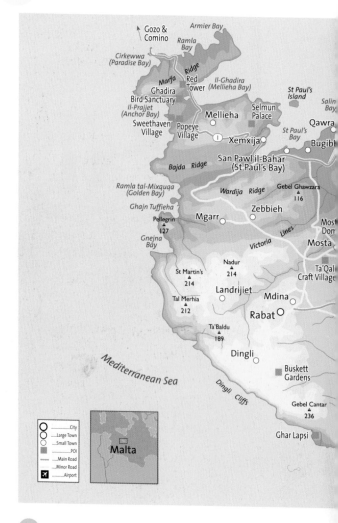

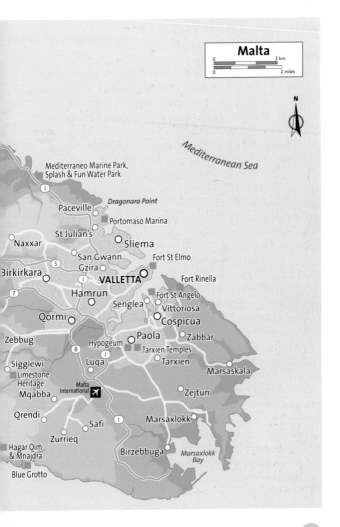

Malta

0 ————— 3 km
0 ————— 2 miles

N

Mediterranean Sea

Mediterraneo Marine Park,
Splash & Fun Water Park

Paceville   *Dragonara Point*

Portomaso Marina

St Julian's

Naxxar   Sliema

San Gwann   Fort St Elmo

Birkirkara   Gzira

VALLETTA   Fort Rinella

Hamrun   Fort St Angelo

Senglea   Vittoriosa

Qormi   Cospicua

Zebbug   Hypogeum   Paola   Zabbar

Tarxien Temples

Siggiewi   Luqa   Tarxien

Limestone
Heritage
Mqabba   Malta
International ✈   Zejtun

Qrendi

Safi   Marsaxlokk

Hagar Qim   Zurrieq
& Mnajdra   Birzebbuga   *Marsaxlokk
Bay*

Blue Grotto

Marsaskala

Getting to know Malta

The Maltese islands form an archipelago in the middle of the Mediterranean. Malta is the largest of the group and by far the most popular as a holiday destination, with well-developed modern resorts, harbours suitable for yachts and cruise liners, and an international airport. Its sister island to the north, Gozo, is smaller, more rural and less developed as a holiday island but has its own attractions that make it worth a visit. In between is the tiny island of Comino, which has a population of fewer than ten and one hotel that is open only during the summer. There are several uninhabited islands: Cominotto, next to Comino; Filfla, a rocky outcrop off the southern coast of Malta; and St Paul's Island, just off the coast at St Paul's Bay in the northeast. Malta is about the size of the Isle of Wight, measuring 21 km (13 miles) long by 14 km (9 miles) wide at its furthest points. Gozo is just 14 km (9 miles) by 6.5 km (4 miles).

The British love affair with Malta goes back over 200 years when a naval force led by Horatio Nelson liberated the island from the tyranny of Napoleon. The British were an integral part of Maltese life from 1800 to 1979, and British influences are still visible. Most Maltese speak English fluently. Malta gained its independence in 1964 and became a republic in 1974, but remains a member of the Commonwealth. It is now also a member state of the European Union with the euro as its currency.

Although Malta is famous today as a laid-back sunshine holiday destination it has a turbulent past. Not just once, but twice, events on this tiny rock have shaped the course of world history. First was the Great Siege of Malta in 1565, when Malta became the decisive battleground in the conflict between Islam and Christianity. A force of 40,000 Turks fought the Maltese defenders and the Crusader Knights of St John, who had made Malta their base. After huge losses on both sides, the Ottoman Empire was defeated. Such was the gratitude of the Pope and European kings that Malta was rewarded with riches that helped endow it with the country churches and official buildings that are still very much in evidence today. Its second period of strategic significance was during World War II, when its geographical position made it the focal point of Mediterranean and North African conflicts. It endured 154 days and nights of blitz, and was recorded as the most bombed place on earth. But the islanders were resilient and Malta continued to operate as a vital supply point for Allied convoys. Britain awarded the island, and by implication every islander, the George Cross, its highest award for civilian gallantry.

🔺 *Azure Window, Gozo*

THE BEST OF MALTA

There is much to explore on Malta and its islands, both by the coast and inland. Discover its rich history and character.

TOP 10 ATTRACTIONS

- **Valletta Waterfront** Take a break, sit for a coffee or have a meal and watch the comings and goings of yachts and cruise ships in Valletta's new development (see page 46).

- **St John's Co-Cathedral, Valletta** This is a must-see for the fabulous gold decoration in the chapels designed by the Knights (see page 45).

- **Mdina** Enjoy panoramic views from the town walls across the island and out to sea, and visit the wonderful cathedral (see pages 56–61).

- **Ta'Qali Craft Village** See artisans at work on glass-making, jewellery and ceramics (see page 100).

- **Boat ride** No visit to Malta is complete without a boat ride, and there are plenty to choose from (see pages 83–5).

- **Gozo** The island that is so relaxed that people say time stands still (see page 67).

- **Portomaso** Wander around St Julian's and Paceville's luxury marina (see page 20).

- **Diving** Malta has at least 25 safe diving sites, including shipwrecks, with diving centres catering for all levels of experience (see pages 16, 25, 35 & 105).

- **Mosta Dome** Marvel at the magnificent Mosta Dome, reputed to be the third-largest unsupported dome in Europe (see pages 80–81).

- **The Malta Experience** This audiovisual spectacular in Mdina is a highly entertaining introduction to the history of Malta (see page 41).

● *The impressive façade of Rabat's Domus Romana*

SYMBOLS KEY

The following symbols are used throughout this book:

ⓐ address ☎ telephone ⓕ fax ⓦ website address ⓔ email
🕒 opening times ❶ important

The following symbols are used on the maps:

𝒊 information office		○ city	
✉ post office		○ large town	
✈ airport		○ small town	
✚ hospital		■ point of interest	
⊗ police station		— main road	
⊟ bus station		— minor road	
✝ cathedral			
❶ numbers denote featured cafés, restaurants & evening venues			

RESTAURANT CATEGORIES

The symbol after the name of each restaurant listed in this guide indicates the price of a typical three-course meal without drinks for one person:

£ up to €15   ££ €15–€20   £££ over €20

▶ *Malta is full of historic attractions, like the church in Balzan*

RESORTS
Places under the sun

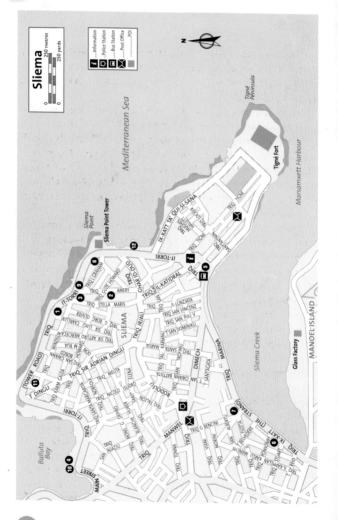

Sliema

0   250 metres
0   250 yards

Information
Police Station
Bus Station
Post Office
POI

N

Mediterranean Sea

Tigné Peninsula

Tigné Fort

Marsamxett Harbour

Sliema Point

Sliema Point Tower

IX-XATT TA' QUI-SI-SANA

TRIQ TIGNÉ

IL-KATIDRAL

SLIEMA

IL-LUNZJATA

TRIQ SAN VINCENZ

TRIQ SAN PIJU V

Y SAN DOMINIKU

Sliema Creek

MANOEL ISLAND

Glass Factory

(THE STRAND)

IX-XATT

Balluta Bay

MAIN STREET

IT-TORRI

DINGLI

TOWER ROAD

TRIQ SIR ADRIAN DINGLI

Sliema

Sliema (pronounced 'Slee-ma') is the fashionable part of Malta, with fine shopping, dining and top-class hotels. It is not only a popular resort but also a much sought-after place to live. An address in Sliema has class and a price tag to go with it.

The town is built on a headland and has two waterfronts, one facing out to the Mediterranean Sea and the other facing Valletta across Marsamxett Harbour with **Manoel Island**, home of the Malta Yacht Club, in between. It's from here that most island boat cruises start, at jetties all along The Strand and Tigné Seafront. From here you can catch buses to Valletta and most other parts of the island. The **Tigné Peninsula**, which juts out pointing towards Valletta, has good places for swimming but there is no beach.

The northern waterfront, Tower Road, has been developed into a charming, tree-lined promenade which stretches all the way to the neighbouring resort of St Julian's. Along this attractive and bustling street you can find numerous cafés, bars and restaurants. At the tip of the headland is **Tigné Fort**, the last of the defences built by the Knights of St John in 1792.

Sliema's shopping centre is between the two waterfronts and is home to international stores such as Marks & Spencer and Stefanel as well as local independent shops and boutiques. Sliema's shops are among the best on the island – look for Maltese lace, fine silverware and pottery. From The Strand there is a bridge over to Manoel Island where there is a **glass-making factory** where artisans blow Phoenician Glass: you can watch exquisite items being made and buy their products in a showroom.

Sliema is also the location of some fine hotels, including the four-star Victoria Hotel and its neighbour, The Palace, a five-star establishment in the town centre. The neighbourhood has numerous attractive Art Nouveau villas, which were built in the early 20th century for wealthy families who were looking to break out of the confines of Valletta.

THINGS TO SEE & DO

Diving

Scubanauts Dive School in the Qui-Si-Sana area of the seafront provides dive trips and diving courses. Their trial scuba dives are very popular with visitors and provide a perfect introduction to the underwater world.
ⓐ Flat 2, 52 St Agatha, Triq St Agatha ⓣ 9925 0372 ⓦ www.maltascuba.com

Harbour tours

A cruise around Valletta and the Three Cities, or taking the ferry across to Valletta, is an unmissable part of anyone's visit to Malta. Boats depart regularly from The Strand. For details, enquire at the booths that line the promenade.

Swimming

Sunbathing and swimming are 'on the rocks' at Sliema. The rocks are smooth and shelve gradually into the sea, running along the north side of the peninsula towards St Julian's. There are public and private lidos along the Qui-Si-Sana and Tower Road, complete with cafés and watersports facilities.

TAKING A BREAK

Cara's Café £ ❶ A popular place for snacks, light meals and pastries, which can have long queues at weekends. The 'Sweets Gallery' is heaven for anyone with a sweet tooth, and you can sip on a yoghurt milkshake in any of ten flavours. ⓐ 249 Tower Road ⓣ 2134 3432

> **SHOPPING**
> On Bisazza Street, pop in to the four-storey **Plaza Shopping Centre**. Here you will find the top international labels all under one roof. ⓛ 09.00–13.00, 16.00–19.00 Mon–Sat

La Cuccagna £ ❷ Casual, family-run restaurant near the sea, serving pizzas, pasta, salads, meats and ribs. The ricotta-filled ravioli is home-made, as are the burgers. Gluten-free pasta and pizzas available on request. ⓐ 47 Triq Amery ❶ 2134 6703 ⓛ Closed Sat lunchtime and Mon evening

Surfside £ ❸ Though it looks like any other Tower Road beachside kiosk, the pizzas, pasta and salads here are delicious and the crowd is usually very lively. Large terrace overlooking the sea. ⓐ Tower Road (opposite New Tower Palace Hotel) ❶ 2134 5384

AFTER DARK

RESTAURANTS
Piccolo Padre £ ❹ Great little pizzeria in the basement of the popular Barracuda (see page 19). A very lively place that's ideal for all ages. Book a seat with views on to scenic Balluta Bay. ⓐ 195 Main Street, Balluta Bay ❶ 2134 4875

Ta'Kris £ ❺ Locals say that 'Dad's Bragioli', made from thin slices of beef rolled and stuffed with minced pork and ham then braised slowly in a tomato and wine sauce, is as close as you can get to Maltese home cooking in a restaurant. ⓐ 80 Fawwara Lane ❶ 2133 7367

Bombay Palace ££ ❻ Unusual because this branch of the Bombay Palace chain is both an Indian and a Chinese restaurant, and both types of food can be served at the same time. Great for a group night out! Part of the Bayview Hotel. ⓐ 143 The Strand ❶ 2132 0216 ⓦ www.bayviewmalta.com

Chez Philippe ££ ❼ A taste of France on the border between Sliema and Gzira. The fare is French provincial; not fancy but wholesome and good. ⓐ 181 The Strand ❶ 2133 0755

Ta'Kolina ££ **❸** A favourite with locals, serving a mixture of Maltese and Italian dishes. Rabbit cooked in wine is a speciality, along with octopus, *bragioli* and home-made ravioli. Portions are generous.
ⓐ 151 Tower Road **☏** 2133 5106

⬤ *The promenade, Sliema*

Tex-Mex Restaurant ££ ❾ Bright Mexican prints and southwestern kitsch adorn this delightful Mexican restaurant that boasts the best margaritas on the island. It also serves Mediterranean-style food. ⓐ 132 Tower Road, opposite the promenade ⓣ 2131 8943 ⓦ www.texmex malta.com

Barracuda £££ ❿ Excellent Mediterranean restaurant specialising in fish and occupying a sturdy 18th-century stone house on the edge of Balluta Bay. Book a table with a waterside view. ⓐ 194 Main Street, Balluta Bay ⓣ 2133 1817

The Kitchen £££ ⓫ Small contemporary restaurant with a modern inventive menu, run by award-winning chef Marc Gauci and his partner Nadja. It's scenically located on the Sliema seafront, with signature dishes including duck breast with glazed pears, and prawn and salmon fillets with a coconut fish sauce. There's also a wonderful selection of vegetarian options. ⓐ 210 Tower Road ⓣ 2131 1112 ⓦ www.thekitchen malta.com

NIGHTLIFE

Venus ⓬ This nightclub is the main entertainment venue in the Preluna Hotel and has a high-tech sound and light system. There is live music most weekends in the Sky Room. ⓐ 124 Tower Road ⓣ 2133 4001 ⓦ www.preluna-hotel.com

PROMENADING

When the sun goes down on Malta, local families come out – as they do all over the Mediterranean region – for a *passegiata* (promenade). One particularly popular spot is along Tower Road. Stalls selling all manner of Maltese snacks and ice creams, and impromptu markets, are set up to catch the passing trade.

St Julian's & Paceville

St Julian's has grown from being a small, sheltered fishing village into one of Malta's biggest and busiest resorts. Fishing still goes on, and in **Spinola Bay** and **St George's Bay** the traditional brightly coloured fishing boats known as *luzzus* (pronounced 'lut-sues') compete for space among pleasure craft.

The traditional centre of St Julian's is the area around Spinola Bay in Portomaso, which is now a smart yachting marina complex with a new Hilton Hotel and numerous upmarket restaurants and bars. The area is dominated by the landmark **Portomaso Business Tower**, an office block resplendent in bold terracotta and deep blue.

Between Spinola Bay and St George's Bay is Paceville (pronounced 'Parch-ay-vill'), the nightlife capital of Malta, chock-a-block with bars and nightclubs. It seems quite mellow in the daytime, when most attention is paid to the **Bay Street Complex**, a multi-storey shopping and entertainment centre. Most nights of the week, but especially at weekends, the area comes alive with loud music and is buzzing until the early hours with crowds of young people from all over the island.

At the northern end of St Julian's is St George's Bay, which has a small sandy beach and places to eat and drink in a more relaxed and quiet atmosphere. The hill beside the bay has several upmarket hotel developments. At the tip of the headland is Dragonara Point, where Malta's largest casino is located in the **Dragonara Palace**, an ornate 19th-century mansion behind the Westin Dragonara Resort Hotel.

THINGS TO SEE & DO

Most sunbathing in the St Julian's area is done at lidos found along the coastline or around the pools within resort hotel complexes. One of the best lidos is the Reef Club, an exclusive beach club offering a selection of watersports, including waterskiing and windsurfing.

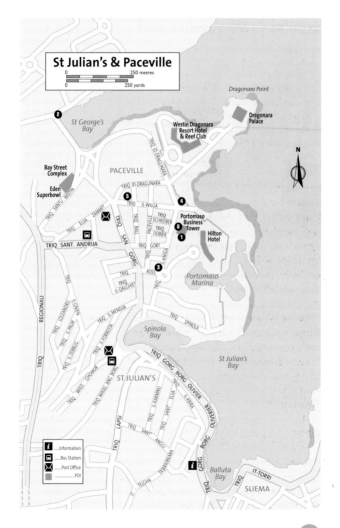

🔺 *Spinola Bay, St Julian's*

Divewise

Scuba-diving school within the Westin Dragonara resort complex, with a waterfront location, pools and sheltered areas where most of the training dives take place. ❶ 2135 6441 ⓦ www.divewise.com.mt ⓔ info@divewise.com.mt

Eden SuperBowl

Tenpin bowling centre with 20 lanes. ⓐ St George's Road, Paceville ❶ 2371 0777 ⓦ www.edensuperbowl.com ⓔ superbowl@edenleisure.com

TAKING A BREAK

Caffé Portomaso £ ❶ Located at the base of the Portomaso Business Tower, Malta's only skyscraper, this is a great place for a coffee, sandwich,

pizza or salad, and there's a vast range of cakes. ⓐ Portomaso
ⓣ 2137 1238 ⓛ 09.00–23.00 daily

Andrew's Bar/Indri's Restaurant ££ ❷ Unpretentious and serving
home-cooked fresh fish. The restaurant has been run by the family for
four generations in a former blacksmiths' forge at the head of St
George's Bay. Maltese, Italian and English dishes are served all day. The
vegetable soup is divine and the lobster platter superb. Try to catch
the fish soup – it's not on every day. ⓐ St George's Bay, St Julian's
ⓣ 2138 8031 ⓦ www.andrewsbar.com ⓛ Hours vary

AFTER DARK

RESTAURANTS
Buffalo Bill's ££ ❸ American-themed steakhouse and a meat-eater's
paradise. The bar area is done out like a cowboy saloon from a
Hollywood film set, but the tables on the terrace are more genuinely
Mediterranean. Parking is free. ⓐ Portomaso Marina ⓣ 2138 9290
ⓦ www.buffalobillsteakhouse.com ⓛ Hours vary

La Maltija ££ ❹ One of the few restaurants in the area serving only
traditional Maltese food. The building is an old town house that used to
be occupied by British officers serving on Malta. ⓐ 1 Church Street,
Paceville ⓣ 2135 9602 ⓦ www.lamaltija.com ⓛ 18.00–23.00 daily

NIGHTLIFE
Coconut Grove and Remedy Rock Bar ❺ Large, popular nightclub
offering a choice of rock and metal music. Interesting cocktail menu
and good coffee. ⓐ 17 Triq Il-Wilga, Paceville ⓣ 2135 3385
ⓦ www.coconut.com.mt ⓛ 19.00–04.00 daily ⓘ Age 17+ only

Twenty Two ££ ❻ Stylish cocktail bar on the top floor of the Portomaso
Business Tower, with panoramic views over the whole island.
ⓐ Portomaso ⓣ 2310 2222 ⓦ www.22.com.mt ⓛ Hours vary

Bugibba & Qawra

Together, Bugibba (pronounced 'Boo-jib-a') and Qawra (pronounced 'Aw-rah') form one of Malta's most important holiday areas. The former consists mainly of apartments, while the latter comprises a handful of large hotels with panoramic views on to **Salina Bay**. Both resorts have modern, pedestrianised centres with shops, restaurants and bars catering mainly to British tastes.

At Bugibba, a long promenade runs along the waterfront overlooking the lido, offering access to the sea, cafés and a funfair. Nightlife is lively with numerous late-night bars and discos. Qawra is somewhat quieter, and has good watersports facilities. Amid all the modern tourist facilities there are two remnants of the era of the Knights.

Qawra Tower at the tip of the peninsula was built by the Grand Master Martin de Redin in the 17th century. At the head of Salina Bay is a curious expanse of shallow square depressions cut into the rock. These are salt pans carved out by the Knights in the 17th century and they are still used commercially.

BEACHES & LIDOS

George's Seafront A public beach lido open to all, spread over two levels. On the upper section there is a bar and restaurant, and the lower level has a pool, sundeck and access to the sea. **❸** Island Promenade, Bugibba

Sunny Coast Popular lido where you can play tennis, use the gym or indoor pool, or simply relax on the sundeck. **❸** Qawra Road

THINGS TO SEE & DO

Malta Classic Car Collection
Paradise for lovers of classic cars. The collection was built up over 15 years by the owner, Mr Carol Galea, and is displayed in a museum. A bubble car, a Mini Cooper, a Corvette and a Thunderbird are among the classics.

The museum has a cinema screening films of the golden years of Grand Prix motor racing and classic car films. ⓐ Klamari Street, Qawra ❶ 2157 8885 ⓦ www.classiccarsmalta.com ⓔ info@classiccarsmalta.com ❶ 09.30–18.00 Mon–Fri, 09.30–13.30 Sat, closed Sun

Mermaid Cruises

This award-winning company organises day trips to Comino and the Blue Lagoon (see page 77). Captain Pawlu sets off in his *luzzu* from the Bugibba jetty every day in the tourist season at 11.00, returning at 17.00. ⓐ 181 St Simon Street, Bugibba ❶ 9957 4438

Oracle Casino

Take a chance and win some money at poker or roulette, or throw it away in state-of-the-art slot machines. Dress code is smart casual. ⓐ Qawra Seafront ❶ 2157 0057 ⓦ www.oraclecasino.com ⓔ win@ oraclecasino.com ❶ Passport required for entry

Subway Dive Centre

Diving school offering PADI approved courses from beginner to instructor level. Subway can help to find accommodation nearby if you want to devote your whole time on Malta to diving. ⓐ Vista Complex, Pioneer Road, Bugibba ❶ 2157 2997 ⓦ www.subwayscuba.com ⓔ info@ subwayscuba.com

AFTER DARK

RESTAURANTS

All Saints £ Situated on the seafront with unobstructed views, this restaurant features Mediterranean cuisine and is one of the best places in Qawra for a drink and a pizza. Very popular with locals and visitors. ⓐ Qawra Road ❶ 2157 3104 ❶ Hours vary

Churchill's £ Casual, relaxed dining in attractive surroundings and very reasonably priced. The menu is Maltese and Mediterranean, with a huge

choice of pasta, meats and fresh fish of the day. ⓐ Il-Fliegu Street, Qawra
ⓣ 2157 2480 ⓛ 18.30–22.30 Tues–Sun, closed Mon

Paderborn £ A cosy restaurant serving Italian and Sicilian-style dishes,
pasta and pizzas in a quiet street close to the seafront. Local fish and
steaks are cooked well. ⓐ Gifen Street, Bugibba ⓣ 2158 1205
ⓛ Hours vary

Incognito ££ A good standard of Maltese and international dishes is on
the menu at this highly popular bar-restaurant. Flambéed dishes are a
speciality. Live music and entertainment nightly. ⓐ Il-Fliegu Street, Qawra
ⓣ 2157 2028 ⓛ Hours vary

Luzzu ££ Popular and casual open-plan restaurant on the Qawra
seafront, serving sandwiches, pizzas, pasta, steaks and fish. ⓐ Qawra
Road ⓣ 2158 4647 ⓛ 18.00–23.00 Mon, 12.00–23.00 Tues–Sun (summer)

● *Qawra Tower and the amazing beach formations*

Ta'Cassia Salina ££ Located in a delightful old house set in its own grounds, close to the salt pans on the coast road to St Paul's Bay. The menu is Maltese and international and you can eat outdoors in the rambling garden. The suckling pig is to die for. ⓐ Tri il-Katatombi, Salina ⓣ 2157 1435 ⓦ www.tacassia.com ⓛ 19.00–late daily

NIGHTLIFE

There are numerous pubs in Bugibba that offer entertainment, especially pool and karaoke. Try The English Bar in St Simon Street, or Paul's Cactus Bar in St Anthony Street. In Qawra, British-style pubs are clustered in the streets near the bus station.

Amazonia A beach club converted into a series of themed bars and discos. One of the top nightspots on the island. ⓐ The Promenade (opposite the Oracle Casino), Qawra ⓣ 2158 1510

Billabong Bar A well-stocked bar with a wide selection of cocktails right in the heart of Qawra. Snacks including home-made pastries available. A big-screen TV shows live football, rugby, boxing and Formula 1. ⓐ 28 Andrew Cunningham Street, Qawra ⓣ 2157 1470

De Niro's As the name suggests, the bar is themed around the actor Robert De Niro and his image adorns the walls. Serves a wide selection of drinks, cocktails and shooters at very reasonable prices. Party nights are hosted by some of the island's top DJs. ⓐ Julio Street, Bugibba ⓣ 2158 1941

Fuego Salsa Bar Very popular venue for Latin music and dancing, attracting a broad age range. Located on the coast road, a short walk from the main promenade of Bugibba and Qawra. DJs play a mix of commercial and pure Latin, keeping the party going till dawn. ⓐ Qawra Coast Road, Qawra ⓣ 2138 6746 ⓦ www.fuego.com.mt ⓛ 22.30–04.00 daily ⓘ Age 18+ only (ages 13–17 19.30–22.30 in summer)

St Paul's Bay

Local tradition has it that St Paul's Bay (San Pawl il-Bahar) is the site where the Apostle Paul was shipwrecked while on his way to trial in Rome in AD 60. He was washed ashore (together with St Luke) and so brought Christianity to Malta. Today the little fishing settlement of St Paul's Bay is largely unaffected by tourism, which has its focus a short distance around the bay, at Bugibba and Qawra (see pages 24–7).

The harbour, with its bright fishing boats bobbing peacefully in the water, is one of the most picturesque spots on the island. On the shore

⬤ *The harbour at St Paul's Bay*

near the town centre is the **Wignacourt Tower**, built by a Grand Master
in 1610, which now houses a small exhibition about Malta's heritage as
an island fortress. ⏰ 09.00–12.00 Mon–Fri, closed Sat & Sun

Out in the bay is St Paul's Island, which is split into two parts, the
larger of which boasts a statue. The island can be seen on a boat trip
round the bay, running from the quay at Bugibba, a short walk away. On
the opposite side of the bay to St Paul's is **Xemxija** (pronounced 'Shem-
shee-ya'), meaning 'Sunny Place', also with some access to the sea. Beyond
is **Mistra Bay**, a secluded sandy and pebbly inlet. If you want to sunbathe,
a much better idea is to visit the lovely sandy beaches of **Golden Bay** and
Ghajn Tuffieha (pronounced 'Ein-tuff-ee-ha') just 6 km (4 miles) west.
Beware – they do get very busy in high season and at weekends. Near
these beaches are the remains of prehistoric temples, the Roman Baths
and the village of Mgarr, with its large church.

BEACHES

The resorts of Bugibba and Qawra are now considered part of St Paul's
Bay and are reached easily by the coast road and regular bus routes.
There is a small beach at the head of St Paul's Bay itself, but most of the
coast in these parts is rocky. Regular buses also run to the sandy beaches
of Mellieha Bay, 8 km (5 miles) away.

THINGS TO SEE & DO

Mgarr Church
This handsome Baroque church is known as the 'Egg Church', as it was
funded largely by the sale of eggs from the village – hence also its
strange egg-shaped dome (which is best appreciated from a distance).
ⓐ Mgarr town centre

Mgarr Shelter
Mgarr's World War II underground shelter, opened to the public in 2003,
is one of the island's largest; 12 m (39 ft) deep and more than 225 m

(738 ft) long, it was dug entirely by hand. Oddly, the entrance is through a restaurant which serves Maltese food – with rabbit stew a speciality!
ⓐ Barri Restaurant, Church Square ① 2157 3235 ② Shelter: 09.00–13.00 Tues–Sat, 10.00–13.00 Sun, closed Mon; restaurant: 09.00–14.30 Tues–Sat, 10.00–15.00 Sun, closed Mon ⓦ www.il-barri.com.mt

Roman Baths

The remains of the steam rooms, hot and cold baths, swimming pool and mosaics uncovered at this ancient villa are proof that the pursuit of leisure has a long history on Malta. The ruins are visible through the fence, but for access the Museums Department requires advance notice.
ⓐ Just over 1.5 km (nearly 1 mile) from Ghajn Tuffieha on the road to Mgarr ① 2145 4125 ② Office hours 09.00–16.00

Skorba Temples

A Neolithic village was uncovered here, and pottery from the site can be seen in the National Museum of Archaeology in Valletta. The remnants of the two temples are contemporary with Ggantija on Gozo and thought to be the oldest free-standing structures in the world. ⓐ About 1.5 km (1 mile) east of Mgarr, on the outskirts of Zebbieh ① 2158 0590 ② Guided tours 09.00–12.00 Tues, Thur & Sat ① Admission charge

AFTER DARK

RESTAURANTS

The Fortress £ Wine bar offering an impressive range of international platters – Maltese, Greek, Chinese and Mexican among them. An outdoor terrace lounge is furnished with white leather armchairs and sofas and has a view across Xemxija Bay. ⓐ Coast Road, Xemxija Bay ① 7901 5757 ② Hours vary

Portobello ££ Located on the hillside overlooking St Paul's Bay and facing westwards, so the sunsets make for a truly romantic evening meal. The restaurant specialises in pasta and fresh fish, and there are chef's

THE SERPENT AND THE SAINT
The parish church, **St Paul's Shipwreck**, is said to be built on the spot where the Apostle was bitten by a deadly viper. Apparently unaffected, he threw the snake into the fire beside him, thus enhancing his already saintly reputation.

specials every day. The home-made soups are divine. ⓐ St Luke's Street ⓣ 7988 8840 ⓛ Hours vary

Shaukiwan ££ The best Chinese food in the area, set in a quiet and romantic location, overlooking Xemxija Bay. ⓐ Xemxija Hill ⓣ 2157 3678 ⓛ 19.00–24.00 daily, also 12.00–16.00 Sun

Zeus ££ A classic Greek restaurant on the main road from St Paul's Bay to Mellieha. ⓐ Xemxija Hill ⓣ 2157 8585 ⓛ 19.00–23.00 daily, also 12.00–15.00 Sun (winter)

Gillieru £££ One of the area's best restaurants, specialising in fish and seafood – especially lobsters and shellfish – and local dishes. This is the place to splurge on a seafood platter or a special seafood pasta with sea urchins. Eat inside or on the terrace for wonderful views over the bay. ⓐ 66 Church Street ⓣ 2157 3269/3480 ⓦ www.gillieru. com.mt ⓛ 12.30–14.30, 19.30–23.00 daily ⓘ Reservations recommended

Porto del Sol £££ Fish, seafood and Maltese dishes are on the menu at this upmarket restaurant. Try the rack of lamb, or breast of duck with a sweet curry sauce, followed by fresh fruit pavlova. Superb location with large windows that make the most of the panoramic bay views. Sunday lunch is highly recommended. ⓐ Xemxija Road ⓣ 2157 3970 ⓦ www.portodelsolmalta.com ⓛ Hours vary

Mellieha

Mellieha Bay (pronounced 'Mell-ee-ha') is famous for its white sandy beach – easily the longest on the island at around 600 m (655 yds). It shelves gently into the Mediterranean and is nearly always a colourful sight, with yachts and *luzzus* at anchor while windsurfers skim the waves. The unspoilt village of Mellieha is perched high above the beach with its landmark parish church looking imperiously down on the seaside activity.

The road sweeps dramatically up from the beach to **Marfa Ridge**, the northernmost part of the island. This is good walking country, although you can also drive to the northern and southern extremities for dramatic sea views; on a clear day, the islands of **Comino** and **Gozo** seem almost within swimming distance. Side roads descend to the lesser-known beaches of **Armier Bay**, **Paradise Bay** and **Ramla Bay**, and ferries depart from Cirkewwa for the island of Gozo (see page 67). On a summer weekend the roads to and from Mellieha are chock-a-block with Maltese beachgoers. If you want to avoid the worst of the crowds, get there early or late – most families will leave around 17.00, even though there will be sunshine for hours to come.

BEACHES

Malta's best sandy beaches are in the north, but all are generally quite small and can get crowded. Not far from Mellieha Bay are three superb sandy beaches: **Golden Bay**, which is truly beautiful, set in a bay between cliffs; **Gnejna Bay** (pronounced 'Je-nay-na'), a sandy beach with fishermen's boathouses, snack bars and some watersports; and **Ghajn Tuffieha**, a sandy cove in a beautiful natural setting, but the beach is narrow and often becomes crowded.

Armier Bay This small but attractive sandy beach is used mostly by locals and may provide a less crowded alternative when Mellieha Beach gets too busy – but don't bank on it!

Mellieha Bay (Il-Ghadira) Many visitors consider this to be Malta's finest beach. Most watersports are catered for, but the conditions particularly favour windsurfing.

Paradise Bay (Cirkewwa) This lovely sandy cove lies behind the Gozo ferry terminal and is something of a secret to many visitors. On a summer weekend, however, it is packed to the gills with local people.

Ramla Bay This sandy cove is another alternative on the north coast of the Marfa Ridge, though it often catches a swell.

◆ *For a small island, Malta has a lot of fine architecture*

THINGS TO SEE & DO

Adira Sailing Centre & Lido

Sailing school and lido on the outskirts of Mellieha, with RYA-certified instructors. Boards and dinghies available at reasonable rates. ⓐ Marfa Road, Mellieha Bay ⓣ 9951 5360

Ghadira Bird Sanctuary

This bird sanctuary in Mellieha is one of two wetlands in northern Malta that have been declared Special Areas of Conservation. ⓣ 2134 7646 ⓦ www.birdlifemalta.org ⓔ info@birdlifemalta.org ⓛ 10.00–16.00 Sat & Sun, other times by appointment

Golden Bay Horse Riding

Very friendly stables at Golden Bay, located close to the Radisson Blu hotel. Rides suitable for all ages, including visits to Sweethaven Village. A sunset ride to the coast overlooking the Gozo Channel is a popular option. Well signposted from the bus stop for routes 652 and 47 at Golden Bay. ⓣ 2157 3360 ⓦ www.goldenbayhorseriding.com ⓔ jfrendo@gmail.com ⓛ 07.00–21.00 daily (summer); 09.00–17.00 daily (winter)

Our Lady of the Grotto Chapel

This small, cave-like chapel is one of the oldest places of worship on the island. Local legend has it that St Paul prayed here. Its frescoes date from around the 11th century. The waters of the underground spring are said to have miraculous powers to heal childhood diseases. The steps leading down into the grotto are lined with letters and photos sent by people who have prayed for and received healing. ⓐ Off Main Street, Mellieha

Red Tower

Perched on the ridge overlooking Mellieha Bay, the Red Tower was built in the 17th century to guard and watch over the northern coastline in order to warn the Knights in Valletta and Mdina of enemy attack. ⓛ 10.00–16.00 Tues, 10.00–13.00 Wed–Mon

Seashell Dive Centre

Scuba diving for everybody, from complete beginners to advanced divers to instructor qualifications. PADI and SSI courses are run every day and the regular programme includes boat, cave, reef and wreck dives. ⓐ Sea Bank Complex, Mellieha Bay ⓣ 2152 2595 ⓦ www.seashell-divecove.com ⓛ 08.00–17.00 Mon–Sat, 08.00–15.00 Sun

Selmun Palace

This handsome 18th-century palace has been restored and is now part of a hotel complex, though non-residents may use its French restaurant. It's worth the detour just to admire its frontage. ⓐ Selmun, Mellieha

Sweethaven Village

Built for the 1980 film *Popeye*, this film set, resembling a ramshackle Newfoundland fishing village, continues to pack in the crowds. The village was built in a photogenic spot, facing a beautiful bay with a tiny sandy beach. **Popeye Village** – a small children's amusement park – has also sprung up here. ⓐ Anchor Bay ⓣ 2152 4782 ⓦ www.popeyemalta.com ⓔ info@popeyemalta.com ⓘ Admission charge

AFTER DARK

RESTAURANTS

Crosskeys £ Bar and restaurant serving good-value meat, chicken and pasta dishes. It also offers takeaway pizzas and serves as a lively karaoke pub. ⓐ Cross Square, Mellieha ⓣ 2152 3744 ⓛ 18.00–23.00 Tues–Sun, closed Mon

L'Amigo Bar & Restaurant ££ A good selection of grilled or fried fish, Maltese dishes, chicken, steaks, pizzas and pasta. You should try the rabbit fried in garlic or cooked in red wine. Dine upstairs on the open-air veranda. ⓐ 55 Gorg Borg Olivier Street ⓣ 2152 0822 ⓛ 11.30–14.00, 18.00–23.00 Mon–Sat, closed Sun

Commando Bar & Restaurant ££ This small restaurant is a good place to try Maltese dishes such as *fenek* (rabbit) or *cerna* (grouper) cooked in wine and herbs. Book a day in advance if you want to try *bragioli* (meat cooked in a traditional stew). ⓐ Gorg Borg Olivier Street, in the square beside the church ⓣ 2152 3459 ⓛ 09.00–13.00, 18.00–24.00 Tues–Sun, closed Mon

Giuseppe's ££ Small, intimate and very busy with local people. Serves local and Italian dishes. Try the sea bass, cuttlefish or quail. ⓐ Gorg Borg Olivier Street, corner of Santa Liena Street ⓣ 2157 4882 ⓔ mjdiacono@onvol.net ⓛ 19.30–23.00 Mon–Sat, closed Sun

Ta'Peter ££ The décor is rather bland but the Maltese food is tasty and good value. Choose from fresh fish, meat or a set tourist menu. ⓣ 2152 3537 ⓛ 18.00–23.00 Mon–Sat, closed Sun

The Arches £££ One of the island's most upmarket restaurants, serving classic continental and Maltese cuisine. Save up and come here on a special occasion. ⓐ 113 Gorg Borg Olivier Street ⓣ 2152 3460 ⓦ www.thearchesmalta.com ⓛ 19.00–late daily

NIGHTLIFE

Mellieha Bay is primarily a beach resort, and those looking for lively evenings should head to **St Julian's** and **Paceville**. The **Limelight** bar and nightclub in the Mellieha Bay Hotel, however, is open to non-residents.

�🜚 *Mellieha's Red Tower*

Valletta

Valletta

Sir Walter Scott called Valletta 'a city built by gentlemen for gentlemen'. The gents in question were the Knights of St John, who built this wonderful city of honey-coloured stone some 430 years ago. Remarkably, it was built in just five years, following the Great Siege of 1565, as the Knights hurried to establish a new fortified capital before the next Turkish onslaught.

Valletta is named after its founder, the Grand Master Jean Parisot de la Vallette. It stretches for nearly 1 km (½ mile) along the hilly peninsula that separates Grand Harbour and Marsamxett Harbour. The best way to appreciate the grandeur of this great walled city and its enormous bastions is on a harbour tour (see page 83).

Valletta is easily explored on foot, as it was laid out in a grid pattern. **Republic Street** is the main central thoroughfare, running from **Fort St Elmo** at the tip of the peninsula to the **Triton Fountain** by the City Gate. Flights of stone steps worn smooth over the centuries lead up and down the steep and atmospheric side streets of the old town, which are lined with tall limestone houses sporting enclosed balconies, small shops and bars. They open on to grand central squares and shady gardens overlooking the sea.

Five of the eight original *auberges*, the palatial inns that housed the different *langues*, or nationalities, of the Order of St John, have survived. The **Auberge de Castille et Léon**, at Castille Place, has the grandest façade and is now the office of the prime minister. The **Auberge d'Italie** in Merchants Street (Triq Il-Merkanti) now houses the Malta Tourism Authority, while the Auberge de Provence is home to the **National Museum of Archaeology**. There are a number of churches worth visiting, including **St Paul's Shipwreck Church**, with frescoed ceilings and a relic of the saint; **La Vittoria** (Church of Our Lady of Victories), Valletta's oldest building; and the **Carmelite Church**, its massive dome a prominent landmark.

Valletta has its own rhythms: surging with shoppers and sightseers during the morning and late afternoon, snoozing during the siesta hours. And today's city is developing a new lease of life at night, with

> ### THE MALTESE CROSS
> The Maltese Cross became the symbol of the Order of the Knights of St John in the mid-13th century. It is white, the colour of purity, and its four arms stand for the virtues of Justice, Fortitude, Prudence and Temperance. The eight points are given different interpretations; a common one is that they represent the Beatitudes from Christ's Sermon on the Mount.

restaurants and wine bars opening in the narrow streets of the city centre and the Valletta Waterfront development near the cruise-liner terminal.

THINGS TO SEE & DO

Casa Rocca Piccola

This 16th-century *palazzo* was built for the Italian knight Pietro La Rocca, and is now the home of his descendant, the 9th Marquis de Piro, himself a modern-day knight. Its rooms contain a rich collection of antique furniture, silver and paintings, and along with the costume museum give a fascinating insight into the customs and lifestyle of the Maltese nobility over 400 years. ⓐ 74 Republic Street ⓣ 2123 1796 ⓦ www.casaroccapiccola.com ⓔ enquiries@casaroccapiccola.com ⓛ Guided tours every hour 10.00–16.00 Mon–Sat ⓘ Admission charge

Grand Masters' Palace

Built in 1571, this splendid palace was home to the Grand Masters of the Knights for over 200 years. Today it is the office of the president of Malta and seat of the country's parliament. The Armouries hold a great collection of military hardware and a lively tour brings the State Apartments to life. ⓐ Entrance on Merchants Street ⓣ 2122 1221 ⓛ 09.30–16.30 daily; State Apartments closed Thur ⓘ Admission charge

Lascaris War Rooms

This warren of underground rooms, within 17th-century tunnels, was the Allied forces' command headquarters during World War II. Operation rooms have been re-created and an audio tour tells the story of the dark days of 1942 when Malta was under siege. ⓐ Lascaris Ditch (well signposted along Valletta's streets) ● 09.30–16.30 Mon–Fri, 09.30–12.30 Sat & Sun ❶ Admission charge

The Malta Experience

This tourist attraction is probably the best of Malta's many audiovisual shows, providing an entertaining general introduction to the island's history and culture. ⓐ St Elmo Bastions, Mediterranean Street ❶ 2124 3776 Ⓦ www.themaltaexperience.com ● Show times on the hour 11.00–16.00 Mon–Fri, 11.00–13.00 Sat & Sun ❶ Admission charge

● The dining table at Casa Rocca Piccola is laid out in grand style

Manoel Theatre

Built by the Knights in 1731–2, this ornate theatre with its beautiful gilded ceiling and tiered boxes was restored in 1960 and again in 2003. Attending a performance here is a treat. ⓐ Old Theatre Street ⓣ 2122 2618 ⓦ www.teatrumanoel.com.mt ⓛ Guided tours 10.15, 11.00, 11.45, 12.30, 13.15, 14.00 Mon–Fri, 12.30 Sat; theatre season Oct–May ⓘ Admission charge

National Museum of Archaeology

Artefacts from Malta's many prehistoric temples and burial sites have been gathered here. Of special interest are the curious statues of fat women, thought to be fertility symbols. ⓐ Auberge de Provence, Republic Street ⓣ 2122 1623 ⓛ 08.00–18.30 daily ⓘ Admission charge

National Museum of Fine Arts

The collection of paintings ranges from the early Renaissance to modern times. Of particular interest are works by Mattia Preti, the Italian Baroque artist who carried out a lot of the church decoration for the Knights in the 17th century. There is also a collection of artefacts and fine silverware including medical equipment used by the Knights in their hospitals. Later works reflect the changes in governance of Malta, and the highlight of the 19th-century section is a Turner watercolour of Grand Harbour. ⓐ South Street ⓣ 2122 5769 ⓔ info@heritagemalta.org ⓛ 09.00–16.30 daily ⓘ Admission charge

National War Museum

Among the World War II memorabilia on display are the actual George Cross awarded to Malta in 1942 by King George VI, *Faith* (a restored Gloster Gladiator biplane), and an Italian E-boat. Audiovisual displays and a vast collection of photographs show the hardships endured by the civilian population during the bombardment of Malta and the extensive damage caused to Valletta and the surrounding towns by Italian and German bombers in 1942. ⓐ Lower Fort St Elmo, Spur Street ⓣ 2122 2430 ⓛ 09.00–17.00 daily ⓘ Admission charge

SHOPPING

Republic Street is the city's main shopping thoroughfare and there is a daily morning market in Merchants Street. The Sunday Market just outside the City Gate has fallen into the tourist trap with tacky plastic souvenirs, beach towels and T-shirts outnumbering the genuine craftworks on sale.

The Artisans Centre Has a good selection of quality jewellery, prints and handicrafts. ⓐ 288 Republic Street, opposite McDonalds ⓘ 2124 6216 ⓛ 09.00–19.00 Mon–Fri, 09.00–18.00 Sat, 11.00–13.00 Sun

Embassy Complex Malta's first shopping mall and entertainment complex, with six floors of retail space, a bingo hall, eating places and a six-screen cinema. Cinema 2 has regular presentations of *Malta GC – The Wartime Experience* (stills and archive movie clips telling the story of Malta in World War II). ⓐ St Lucia Street, just off Republic Street ⓘ 2122 7436 ⓦ www.embassycomplex.com.mt ⓛ 09.00–23.00 Mon–Fri, 14.00–23.00 Sat & Sun

Galea Paintings Artist Aldo Galea's prints and watercolours of Maltese scenes are unique souvenirs of the island. ⓐ 70 South Street & 192 Strait Street ⓘ 2123 7455 ⓛ 09.30–13.00, 16.00–19.00 Mon–Fri, 09.15–12.45 Sat

The Silversmith's Shop Sells plain and filigree silver jewellery. ⓐ 218 Republic Street ⓘ 2123 1416 ⓛ 10.00–17.00 Mon–Fri, 10.00–15.00 Sat, 10.00–13.00 Sun

Re-enactments

In Guardia and *Alarme!* are historical re-enactments of full-scale military parades held on Sundays at Fort St Elmo at 11.00, depicting the defences

Valletta has grand streets with elegant architecture

of Valletta in the days of the Knights and the later French occupation.
🅐 Fort St Elmo 🕿 2123 7747 ❶ Admission charge

La Sacra Infermeria

The 'Holy Infirmary' hospital was built by the Knights in 1574 and
reflects their original function as Knights Hospitallers, caring for sick
and injured pilgrims in the Middle Ages. It is now occupied by 'The
Knights Hospitallers', a series of historical tableaux about the Knights.
🅐 Mediterranean Street 🕿 2122 3840 🕓 10.00–15.30 daily ❶ Admission
charge

St John's Co-Cathedral

So-called because it has equal status with St Paul's Cathedral in Mdina,
which is the seat of the Archbishop of Malta and administrative
headquarters of the island's Catholic Church. This magnificent church
was built in the 1570s, originally as the main place of worship for the
Knights of St John. Grand Masters of the Order are buried in tombs
under the marble floor. The cathedral has eight side chapels, each one
dedicated to a *langue*, or nationality, of the noblemen who made up the
Knights' fraternity. The chapels have been restored to their former glory
with extensive gilding and refurbishment. The Oratory Museum holds a
Caravaggio masterpiece, *The Beheading of St John the Baptist*, painted
while the young artist was staying on Malta to escape charges of
murder in Rome. His *St Jerome Writing* is also on display. 🅐 St John's
Square (entrance on Republic Street) 🕿 2122 0536 🕓 09.30–16.00
Mon–Fri, 09.30–12.00 Sat, closed Sun ❶ Admission charge. Stiletto-
heeled shoes forbidden, shawls provided for women with bare shoulders

Saluting Battery

Every day at 12.00 a cannon is fired from the old Saluting Battery in
Valletta by volunteers from the Malta Heritage Trust dressed in late
19th-century military uniforms. This event re-creates the daily ritual of
earlier times. The noonday gun signalled the exact hour of the day to
mariners moored in the harbour. This allowed them to accurately

calibrate their ship's timepiece, on which they would depend to find their longitude when at sea. Guided tours of the historic battery are available on the hour at this site. The location is easily reached on foot from the main bus station following directional signs.

Valletta Waterfront

The Valletta Waterfront is a prestigious new development overlooking Grand Harbour, with restaurants, cafés and shops set in refurbished warehouses and workshops. The project is the result of a £15 million investment aimed at regenerating the Grand Harbour quayside into a focal point for entertainment. It stretches about 1 km (½ mile) along Pinto Wharf on the northern shore of the harbour and has quickly become the trendy place to be in the evening in Valletta.

The Waterfront has won international awards for conservation of the architectural heritage and is a popular venue for arts and music events, as well as one of the city's best places to eat or take a stroll. It is the main site for the annual Malta Jazz Festival in July and a wine fair in August.

TAKING A BREAK

Café Barrakka £ ❶ Great for a light alfresco lunch while exploring the sights from Valletta's city fortifications, this café is located just beside the main gate of the Upper Barrakka Gardens. Very reasonably priced snacks, pizzas, Maltese pastries and pasta. The menu has theme nights in the summer (for example, Tuesday is Maltese cuisine, Wednesday and Saturday fresh fish, and Friday is rabbit night with the traditional *fenkata* – rabbit in wine stew – the star attraction). ⓐ Castille Place ❶ 2122 3744 ⓛ 09.00–16.00 daily, also 19.00–22.00 Thur–Sat

Chiaroscuro £ ❷ Smart, modern coffee bar set in an old building, serving light Italian dishes, baguettes, tortilla wraps and an Italian buffet at lunchtime. In the evening it becomes a wine and cocktail bar, with a wine bar and nightclub in the cellars. The building is over 500 years old and was built as a town house by the Knights; it has also seen service as a monastery and a hotel. ⓐ 44 Strait Street ⓛ Hours vary

Inspirations! £ ❸ Coffee shop and a small restaurant within the St James Cavalier Centre for Creativity, an arts centre and exhibition space that is now Malta's national contemporary arts venue. Sandwiches, pastries, fajitas, pizzas and salads, served in an open courtyard where artists meet for working lunches and conversation. ⓐ Pope Pius V Street ⓣ 2124 1224 ⓦ www.inspirations.com.mt ⓛ 09.30–20.00 Mon–Wed, 09.30–23.00 Thur–Sun

San Giovanni £ ❹ Just what you need after looking around the Baroque splendours of St John's Co-Cathedral, this outdoor restaurant is immediately outside the cathedral's exit door. A varied menu of pasta, pizzas, fish dishes and some traditional Maltese favourites such as rabbit stew and chicken breast stuffed with ham, cheese and sun-dried tomatoes. ⓐ St John Square ⓛ Hours vary

Caffé Cordina ££ ❺ A city institution. Take a look inside the beautiful interior of the establishment before pulling up a chair on the square outside. ⓐ Republic Square ⓣ 2123 4385 ⓦ www.caffecordina.com ⓛ 08.00–19.00 Mon–Sat, 08.00–15.00 Sun

Fumia Café ££ ❻ Part of the Manoel Theatre and just the thing for a pre-show snack or a coffee break after touring the splendid theatre. Great selection of cakes and pastries. A meeting place for theatregoers, artists and writers. ⓐ Old Theatre Street ⓛ Hours vary

AFTER DARK

RESTAURANTS

Bocconci £ ❼ Healthy eating is the thing in Malta's first Italian-style Slow Food restaurant. Located in the former kitchen of the palace next door, Casa Rocca Piccola. **Ⓐ** 75–76 Republic Street **Ⓣ** 2123 2505 **Ⓦ** www.casaroccapiccola.com **Ⓛ** Lunch & dinner daily

La Cave £ **❽** This cosy wine cellar below the Castille Hotel serves pasta, pizzas and cheese with wine. **Ⓐ** Castille Square **Ⓣ** 2124 3678 **Ⓛ** 12.00–15.00, 18.00–23.00 Mon–Fri, 18.00–23.00 Sat & Sun

Cocopazzo £ **❾** A small restaurant that promises a big treat, but that's if you can find it. It's located in an office block in a side street. Specials change every week and the fresh seafood includes bream, octopus, snapper and calamari (squid), depending on what the fishermen bring in. **Ⓐ** Valletta Buildings, South Street **Ⓣ** 2123 5706 **Ⓛ** 11.30–14.30, 18.30–22.00 daily

Eddie's Café Regina £ **❿** Enjoy the pizzas, pasta, grilled meats and Maltese dishes – including delicious fresh local fish, octopus and rabbit – at the shady green tables in Republic Square or in the café's cool, air-conditioned interior. **Ⓐ** Republic Square **Ⓣ** 2124 6454 **Ⓛ** 09.00–22.00 daily

Spezzo £ **⓫** A stylish lounge bar and restaurant located in the building that is home to the Civil Service Sports Club. Mediterranean menu including sea-urchin pasta and swordfish ravioli. **Ⓐ** 113 Archbishop Street **Ⓣ** 2122 8500 **Ⓦ** www.spezzorestaurant.com **Ⓛ** Lunch Tues–Sun, dinner Tues–Sat; closed Mon

Blue Room £–££ **⓬** Small, air-conditioned Chinese restaurant with smart blue-and-white décor. Nice variations on standard dishes, such as spicy seafood and tofu served in earthenware pots. **Ⓐ** Republic Street **Ⓣ** 9938 4784 **Ⓛ** 12.00–15.00, 19.00–23.00 Tues–Fri & Sun, 19.00–23.00 Mon & Sat

Nan Yuan ££ **⓮** Stylish Chinese restaurant set in the revitalised Valletta Waterfront, with outside tables on the quay. Specialities are aromatic duck with pancake, and cashew-nut chicken. ⓐ Vault 14, Valletta Waterfront ❶ 2122 5310 ⓛ Lunch & dinner Tues–Sun

Rubino ££ ⓯ One of the best places in Valletta to experience a range of genuine Maltese cuisine. The menu has all the traditional dishes such as fresh rabbit in garlic, wine and bayleaves, and fresh local lamb, along with modern creations using only home-grown and fresh-caught ingredients. ⓐ 53 Old Bakery Street ❶ 2122 4656 ⓦ www.rubino malta.com ⓛ 12.30–14.30 Mon–Fri, 19.30–22.30 Tues–Sat

2-22 £££ ⓰ Extraordinary modern design for a restaurant built into the ancient vaults of the bastion overlooking Marsamxett Harbour. Exquisite seafood, oven-baked salmon and grilled duck breast served in the lounge or on the terrace. ⓐ 222 Great Siege Road ❶ 2733 3222 ⓦ www.two-twentytwo.com ⓔ info@two-twentytwo.com ⓛ 19.30–24.00 daily

The Carriage £££ ⓱ Fine cuisine and grand views over the harbour and rooftops of Valletta make this one of the city's best restaurants. The three-course set menu of the week features Mediterranean cooking. ⓐ 22–25 South Street (take the lift from the lobby of the Valletta Buildings) ❶ 2124 7828 ⓛ 12.00–14.30 Mon–Fri, 19.00–23.00 Fri–Sat, closed Sun

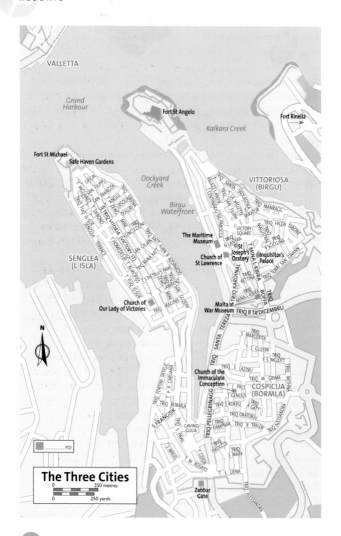

VALLETTA

Grand Harbour

Fort St Angelo

Fort Rinella

Kalkara Creek

Fort St Michael

Safe Haven Gardens

Dockyard Creek

VITTORIOSA (BIRGU)

Birgu Waterfront

The Maritime Museum

St Joseph's Oratory

Church of St Lawrence

Inquisitor's Palace

SENGLEA (L-ISLA)

VICTORY SQUARE

Church of Our Lady of Victories

Malta at War Museum

TRIQ 8 TA'DICEMBRU

N

Church of the Immaculate Conception

COSPICUA (BORMLA)

S. FRANĠISK

Zabbar Gate

POI

The Three Cities

0   250 metres

0   250 yards

The Three Cities

The Three Cities – **Senglea**, **Cospicua** and **Vittoriosa** – occupy the finger-like peninsulas jutting into Grand Harbour from the shore opposite Valletta. They were the first base on Malta for the Knights of St John, who came here in 1530 following their expulsion from Rhodes. Dockyard Creek separates Senglea and Vittoriosa, with Cospicua joining the southernmost points of the two.

The Three Cities are some of Malta's most historic towns, but, because they lack major hotels, restaurants and tourist facilities, visitors generally overlook them. A harbour cruise gives a tantalising glimpse of the handsome waterfront buildings, and of the old-fashioned *dghajsas* (pronounced 'day-sas') – Malta's version of gondolas – drifting peacefully in Senglea's harbour. Anyone who returns to explore the Three Cities in more detail will be rewarded with a taste of Malta as it was in the days before mass tourism.

The Knights first established themselves at Birgu, as Vittoriosa was then known, because it provided shelter for their ships. They set about fortifying the dilapidated Fort St Angelo at the tip of the peninsula and constructing their first *auberges* and palaces. By the 1560s the growing city had spread beyond the walls to form the suburb of Bormla, now known as Cospicua. Meanwhile, the separate town of L-Isla, renamed Senglea after the French Grand Master Claude de la Sengle following the construction of Fort St Michael in 1552, arose on the opposite peninsula. Birgu was renamed Vittoriosa in honour of the Knights' victory over the Turks in the Great Siege of 1565, though many locals still call it by its original name. When the new capital of Valletta was built, the fortunes of the Three Cities began to decline. However, lines of defences continued to be built around them well into the 17th century.

With the development of both the shipbuilding and shipping industries at nearby Marsa, many dockyard workers made their homes in the Three Cities. But they also became targets for bombing raids during World War II, with Senglea and Cospicua in particular suffering extensive damage.

THINGS TO SEE & DO

VITTORIOSA

Vittoriosa has a fine old town centre and is the most atmospheric of the Three Cities. A stroll along its narrow, winding streets reveals many delights, such as the lovely architecture of **Victory Square**, which is surrounded by the *auberges* of England, Germany and Auvergne et Provence. The three elegant gateways on the landward side of the town – Advanced Gate, Couvre Porte and Provence Gate – were built in the early 18th century. The Post of England lookout on the Kalkara Creek side has views of the former Bighi Naval Hospital and the old Ricasoli Fort on adjacent peninsulas.

Church of St Lawrence

This landmark of Vittoriosa's waterfront, with its dome and twin clock towers, is a 17th-century reconstruction of the Knights' original Conventual Church. The interior is richly decorated with red marble, frescoes and an outstanding painting, *The Martyrdom of St Lawrence* by Mattia Preti. In front of the church, the Freedom Monument commemorates the British withdrawal from Malta in 1979. ⓐ St Lawrence Street ⓣ 2182 7057 ⓛ 09.00–12.00, 16.00–18.00 Mon–Sat, closed Sun

Fort St Angelo

The Knights fortified an earlier castle on this strategic point and from here repelled the Turks during the Great Siege. The first Grand Masters and many Knights are buried here. It later became a prison and was a naval base for the Allies during World War II. ⓐ Guided tours every 15 minutes 09.00–13.00 Sat (June–Sept); 10.00–14.00 Sat (Oct–May) ⓘ Admission charge

The Inquisitor's Palace

Built in 1574, this palace was the headquarters of the Inquisition on Malta. Gruesome torture took place here, as the hated inquisitors sought to extract 'confessions' of heresy. The museum contains furniture and household goods. You can also visit the courtroom, main hall, chapel

THE GREAT CHAIN
The Knights had a secret weapon for defending the Three Cities during the Great Siege. An enormous chain, which had been forged in Venice, was strung across the entrance to Dockyard Creek between Senglea and Fort St Angelo. A remnant can still be seen below the fort.

and dungeons, where the prisoners' graffiti are still visible. ⓐ Main Gate Street ⓣ 2182 7006 ⓛ 09.00–16.00 daily ⓘ Admission charge

Malta at War Museum
Small museum dedicated to the civilian struggle during World War II. The main attraction is a guided tour of the underground air-raid shelter. ⓐ Couvre Porte Gate, Vittoriosa ⓣ 2189 6617 ⓛ 10.00–17.00 Tues–Sun, closed Mon ⓘ Admission charge

Maritime Museum
Malta's naval history is illustrated with photos, models of the galleys of the Knights and of traditional Maltese fishing vessels, and even medieval navigation tools. ⓐ The Waterfront ⓣ 2166 0052 ⓛ 09.00–16.30 daily ⓘ Admission charge

St Joseph's Oratory
Built as a chapel behind the Church of St Lawrence in the 18th century, the oratory is now a small museum containing artefacts brought by the Knights from Rhodes. Grand Master Jean de la Vallette's hat and sword, and a crucifix used at executions, are here. ⓐ Victory Square ⓛ 09.30–12.00, 14.00–16.00 Mon–Sat, 09.30–12.00 Sun

COSPICUA
Like neighbouring Senglea, Cospicua was heavily bombed during World War II and there is little to see in its narrow, stepped streets.

The ornate **Church of the Immaculate Conception**, built in 1637, is one of the few buildings to have escaped destruction and is worth a look. The town is enclosed by a double ring of bastions, the landward defences built by the Knights. The inner Margherita Lines, with six bastions, were begun in 1639. Between 1670 and 1680, the Cotonera Lines, funded by Grand Master Nicolas Cotoner, were built beyond. The **Zabbar Gate** is the best of the finely carved triumphal gateways that break the curtain walls.

Fort Rinella

Fort Rinella, built by the British in the 19th century, lies northeast of the Three Cities. It contains the world's largest cannon, the Armstrong 100 ton. Historical re-enactments take place daily during the summer at 14.30. Guided tours on the hour include the firing of a period gun.
ⓐ St Rocco Road, Kalkara (bus 4 from Valletta) ① 2180 9713 ● 09.30–17.00 daily, guided tour 14.30 daily ❶ Admission charge

SENGLEA

Senglea was heavily bombed during World War II. Victory Street, the main thoroughfare, runs from the main square to the gardens on the peninsula. There is also an attractive waterfront along Dockyard Creek.

Church of Our Lady of Victories

The church, in the main town square, was badly damaged in the bombing but is now restored to its former glory, with a fine painted dome.

Safe Haven Gardens

Also called Gardjola Garden, these gardens surround the picturesque *vedette*, or lookout post, on the tip of the peninsula and offer superb panoramic views of the entire Grand Harbour. The *vedette* is a six-sided tower, finely carved with two eyes and two ears to signify vigilance against enemy ships. It is one of the few survivors of pre-World War II Senglea. The gardens were created on the site of Fort St Michael, which was built by the Knights and dismantled by the British to create docks for the Royal Navy.

🔺 *Vittoriosa's waterfront landmark, the Church of St Lawrence*

Medieval Mdina

Malta's old capital is the island's most perfectly preserved medieval town. It is a world away from noisy modern-day resort life, and even the gentle bustle of Valletta is a comparative cacophony. Here in the quiet narrow streets and alleyways you can almost touch the sense of history.

The Romans were the first to settle in this area, attracted, like their successors, by its strategic situation: high inland, easy to defend and surrounded by fertile agricultural countryside. But if the name Mdina (pronounced 'Im-deena') sounds Arabic then that is not surprising. It derives from the word *Medina*, meaning 'the City', and was so named by the Arabs who conquered Malta in 870 and stayed for two centuries, making the city their stronghold and capital.

Sadly, there is virtually nothing left from this period and it was left to the Knights of St John to give Mdina its current form. They fortified the city, made it their cavalry headquarters and called it Città Notabile, meaning 'Eminent City'. The Knights did not stay long, however. After the Great Siege of 1565 they moved to Valletta and so the demise of Mdina began. It became known as 'the Old City' and, as it began to fade away quietly, acquired the name 'the Silent City'.

Thanks to tourism, Mdina is no longer silent – by day at any rate. Restaurants, shops and a handful of attractions draw visitors, and the residents' own motor vehicles disturb the slumber (though no other vehicles are allowed in). At night, however, the town's 400 or so inhabitants enjoy what must be the quietest sleep in all Malta. A visit after dark, when the empty streets fall silent, is highly recommended.

The entrance to the town is through the splendid Main Gate, built in 1724, which lies across a bridge spanning the dry moat. The three statues on the inside façade are of St Publius, St Paul and St Agatha, Malta's three patron saints. Nearly all of Mdina's sightseeing interest lies along the main street, Triq Villegaignon. Walk slowly and gaze upwards to admire the façades of the various *palazzi* (mansions) along here. The most eminent address is Casa Inguanez, the home of Malta's oldest aristocratic family.

⬧ *Main Gate, Mdina*

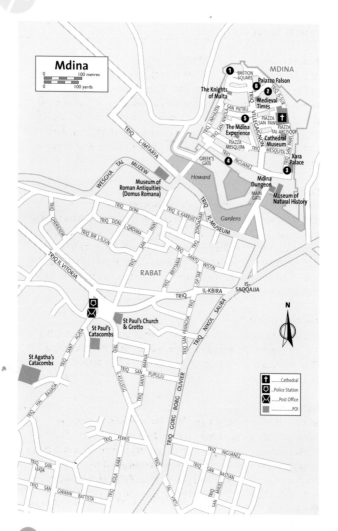

Mdina

0 ___ 100 metres
0 ___ 100 yards

MDINA

① BASTION SQUARE
Palazzo Falson

The Knights of Malta
⑥ ②
Medieval Times
⑤ The Mdina Experience
Cathedral Museum
PIAZZA SAN PAW
PIAZZA TAL-ARCISQOF

GREEK'S GATE
④
Xara Palace
③

Howard

Mdina Dungeon

Museum of Roman Antiquities (Domus Romana)

MAIN GATE

Museum of Natural History

Gardens

RABAT

IS-SAQQAJJA

TRIQ IL VITORIA

TRIQ IL-KBIRA

St Paul's Church & Grotto

St Paul's Catacombs

St Agatha's Catacombs

N

🏛 ....Cathedral
🏢 ...Police Station
✉ ....Post Office
▪ ....POI

THINGS TO SEE & DO

Bastion Square

At the end of Villegaignon Street, Bastion Square makes the perfect end to a stroll through Mdina. From the town walls there are sweeping views across the plains below. Even on the dullest day the giant dome of Mosta's church is a mighty landmark and you should be able to see all the way to Valletta and almost all the way along both coasts towards St Paul's Bay in the north and to Marsaskala in the southeast.

Cathedral Museum

Housed in an 18th-century Baroque palace, this museum features Roman antiquities, a coin collection and numerous works of art, some by famous Old Masters. The highlight is the collection of woodcuts from Albrecht Dürer's *The Small Passion*, depicting important biblical episodes. ⓐ St Paul's Square ⓣ 2145 4697 ⓛ 10.00–16.00 Mon–Fri, 10.00–15.00 Sat, closed Sun ⓘ Admission charge includes a visit to the cathedral

The Knights of Malta

Located in historic gunpowder vaults, a series of tableaux depict the life and times of the Knights accompanied by an audiovisual show. ⓐ 14–19 Magazine Street ⓣ 2145 1342 ⓛ 10.30–16.00 Mon–Fri ⓘ Admission charge

Mdina Dungeon

Some of the scenes in here may look like pure dark fantasy, but these are real dungeons and what you see is an exhibition of real medieval Maltese horror – everything portrayed here actually happened (though not necessarily in these dungeons). If you are squeamish or have young children in tow, give it a miss. ⓐ St Publius Square, just inside the Main Gate ⓣ 2145 0267 ⓛ 09.30–16.30 daily ⓘ Admission charge

The Mdina Experience

This audiovisual show in a comfortable air-conditioned auditorium gives a good general introduction to the history of the city. There is a café on-site. ⓐ 7 Mesquita Square ❶ 2145 4322 ❷ 10.00–16.30 daily ❶ Admission charge

Medieval Times

A series of tableaux depicting medieval life on Malta. ⓐ In the Palazzo Costanzo, Villegaignon Street ❶ 2145 4625 ❷ 09.00–17.00 daily ❶ Admission charge

Museum of Natural History

The handsome 18th-century Vilhena Palace is home to Mdina's old-fashioned natural history museum. It is as dry in tone as some of the bones it displays, but still worth a visit. ⓐ St Publius Square, adjacent to Mdina Dungeon ❶ 2145 5951 ❷ 09.00–17.00 daily ❶ Admission charge

Palazzo Falson

Also known as the Norman House, this beautifully restored 14th-century mansion contains a small museum of naval art and antique furniture, as well as a collection of weaponry. ⓐ Villegaignon Street ❶ 2145 4512 ⓦ www.palazzofalson.com ⓔ info@palazzofalson.com ❷ 10.00–17.00 Tues–Sun, closed Mon ❶ Admission charge (includes audio guide)

St Paul's Cathedral

Built from 1697 to 1702 by Lorenzo Gafà after an earlier church was destroyed by an earthquake, this cathedral is second only to St John's Co-Cathedral in Valletta in grandeur. The rich Baroque interior is one of the finest on Malta; the vaulted ceiling is adorned with frescoes by Mattia Preti, while colourful funerary slabs cover the floor. Other highlights include the high altar of marble and lapis lazuli, and a Byzantine icon of the Madonna and Child in a side chapel. ⓐ St Paul's Square ❶ 2145 4136 ❷ 09.30–16.30 Mon–Sat, 15.00–16.30 Sun ❶ Admission charge combined with ticket to Cathedral Museum

TAKING A BREAK

Ciappetti £ ❶ Charming courtyard restaurant serving Italian specialities, plus traditional rabbit, with a terrace upstairs on the bastion. Gluten-free meals available. ⓐ 5 St Agatha's Esplanade ⓣ 2145 9987 ⓛ 19.00–22.00 Mon–Sat, 12.00–15.00 Sun (summer); 12.00–15.00 daily (winter)

Fontanella £ ❷ Famous for home-made cakes (try the chocolate) and the fantastic view along the ramparts near Bastion Square. Sandwiches and salads are also available. ⓐ 1 Bastion Street ⓣ 2145 4264 ⓛ 10.00–22.30 daily (summer); 10.00–20.00 (winter)

Trattoria AD 1530 £ ❸ Bright trattoria serving pizzas, pasta, grilled meats, fish, salads and light snacks. ⓐ Adjacent to the Xara Palace hotel ⓣ 2145 0560 ⓛ 09.00–22.00 daily

AFTER DARK

RESTAURANTS

Bacchus ££ ❹ Two chambers of a 17th-century gunpowder magazine in one of the town walls' fortified bastions provide a unique setting for one of Mdina's best restaurants. Speciality fish dishes, grills, pasta and salads are on the menu. ⓐ Inguanez Street ⓣ 2145 4981 ⓛ 09.00–23.30 daily

Medina ££ ❺ Located in a house dating back to the 11th century, the best tables are in a vine-covered inner courtyard. The interior has vaulted stone ceilings and in winter there are roaring wood fires. The menu is varied French, Mediterranean and Maltese, and there is a vegetarian selection. ⓐ 7 Holy Cross Street ⓣ 2145 4004 ⓔ info@medinarestaurant.com ⓛ 19.00–22.30 Mon–Sat, closed Sun

Palazzo Costanzo ££ ❻ Coffee shop and restaurant in a beautiful 17th-century Baroque palace. Italian and Mediterranean cuisine, including Maltese dishes. ⓐ Villegaignon Street ⓣ 2745 4625 ⓛ 09.30–17.00 daily

Rabat

Rabat, meaning 'the Suburb' in Arabic, lies just outside Mdina's town walls. The two were one town in Roman times, and became separated when the Arabs began building smaller fortifications around Mdina. Rabat has always acted as the commercial quarter for the old capital.

Rabat is a sprawling town of some 13,000 residents, a commercial hub for much of central Malta. Its main sights, however, are all located around the central Parish Square, about a ten-minute walk from Mdina's historic Main Gate. There is a colourful fruit and vegetable market in the square on weekdays. Few concessions to tourism impinge on the traditional local character of Rabat, and its streets are lined with lovely old-style houses with ornate enclosed balconies. A multitude of saints' statues atop their wooden plinths lines the streets during the annual summer *festa* (town festival).

Rabat is most famous for its early Christian **catacombs** (underground tunnels with niches for tombs). Below the streets lies a subterranean labyrinth, covering more than 2.5 sq km (1 sq mile). Malta's catacombs were used solely as burial chambers, and pagans and Jews were also interred here. There are various types of tomb: floor graves; canopy tombs; and small graves, known as *loculi*, cut into the wall to hold the body of a child.

The most unusual feature of the catacombs is the circular *agape* tables, which were carved out of the rock so that relatives of the dead could gather underground for ritual funeral and anniversary feasts with their departed loved ones. The catacombs are maintained by Heritage Malta; two sets are open to the public.

THINGS TO SEE & DO

Casa Bernard

A 16th-century *palazzo* restored to its original splendour. Not strictly a museum, this is a private family home. Guided tours by the owners take you through splendid drawing rooms, the library, chapel and courtyard.

(a) 43–46 St Paul Street (t) 2145 1888 (e) casabernard@onvol.net
(l) 11.00–15.00 Mon–Sat, closed Sun (!) Admission charge

Domus Romana

Apart from the mosaic floor, little is left of the old Roman villa here,
but the museum built on-site contains an interesting collection of
amphorae (ancient Roman jars), oil lamps, olive crushers and other
artefacts. (a) Museum Esplanade (t) 2145 4125 (l) 09.00–17.00 daily
(!) Admission charge

St Agatha's Catacombs

These catacombs, dedicated to the Sicilian martyr St Agatha, are
outstanding for their late Roman and medieval frescoes. A guide points
out the highlights on a tour lasting 20–30 minutes. There is also a small
museum. (a) St Agatha Street (t) 2145 4503 (l) 09.00–16.30 Mon–Fri,
09.00–12.30 Sat, closed Sun (!) Admission charge

St Paul's Catacombs

Malta's largest catacombs once contained some 1,400 tombs. You
can wander through the eerie maze of lit passages on your own,
starting from a simple chapel near the entrance. (a) St Agatha Street
(t) 2145 4562 (l) 09.00–16.30 daily (!) Admission charge

St Paul's Church & Grotto

Rabat's parish church was built in the 16th century on the site where St
Paul is believed to have taken shelter after being shipwrecked. (a) Parish
Square (t) 2145 4467 (l) 09.00–17.00 Mon–Sat, closed Sun (!) Donation

TAKING A BREAK

The Roadhouse Buskett £ A great place to bring children. The restaurant
is set in Malta's only forest, Buskett Gardens, and serves Italian,
Mediterranean and Maltese food. On Sundays it provides children's
entertainment with a bouncy castle and other outdoor toys. At night the

outside area serves as a nightclub. ⓐ Buskett Gardens, outskirts of Rabat
ⓣ 2145 4233 ⓛ 10.00–04.00 Tues–Sun, closed Mon

Ristorante Cosmana Navarra ££ Stop here during the day for a tasty
snack in the downstairs bar, and return in the evening for the full dinner
menu. Choose from confit duck, rabbit or fish. ⓐ 28 St Paul's Street,
situated opposite the church ⓣ 2145 0638 ⓛ Food 12.00–16.00,
18.30–22.30 daily, bar open until 24.00

AFTER DARK

RESTAURANTS
Jerry's Chopsticks £ A relaxed and unpretentious Chinese restaurant
in Rabat, just outside the gate to Mdina. Classic dishes with a twist, such
as a whole fish with pineapple sauce. ⓐ Saqqajja Square ⓣ 2145 6789
ⓛ 18.30–23.30 Wed–Mon, closed Tues

Roman's Den £ Restaurant and lounge bar with a warm and cosy
atmosphere on the main road through Rabat. ⓐ 58 Main Street
ⓣ 2145 6970 ⓛ 19.00–24.00 Tues–Sun, closed Mon

La Veduta £ The restaurant is perched on top of the hill outside the
walls of Mdina and has stunning views over central Malta towards the
sea. Serving good-value plain food, grills, chicken, pizzas and salads,
La Veduta is popular among Maltese families. ⓐ Saqqajja Square
ⓣ 2145 4666 ⓛ 11.30–15.00, 18.00–23.00 daily

Rogantinos ££ A delightful family-run restaurant in a 16th-century
country lodge on the outskirts of Rabat, towards Mtahleb. The cuisine is
a mixture of Maltese, Italian and French. Specialities include local roast
lamb and suckling pig. ⓐ Wied il-Busbies, Landrijiet ⓣ 2145 2003
ⓛ 19.00–24.00 Tues–Sat, 12.00–16.00 Sun, closed Mon

ⓞ *The historic citadel in Gozo's capital, Victoria*

 EXCURSIONS
Out & about

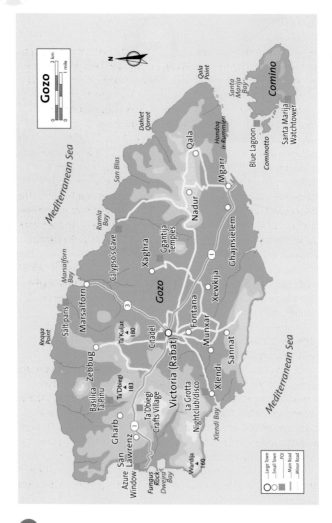

Gozo

Legend has it that Gozo is the mythical island of Calypso, the sea nymph who, in Homer's *Odyssey*, kept Odysseus captive for seven years. You may not stay that long, but you will most certainly feel the ancient attraction of the island's temples, standing stones and time-worn landscapes.

Many visitors wrongly assume that Gozo is just an extension of its larger sister, Malta. Though its villages are built from the same honey-coloured limestone, Gozo has a completely different feel. Guest accommodation is primarily in holiday apartments, farmhouses and upmarket hotels rather than in large resorts, so the atmosphere is quieter and the pace slower. Gozo is Malta's market garden, and its landscape is noticeably greener, especially in the sun-baked summer. The hillsides and valleys are covered with fertile orchards and terraced fields that are still worked using traditional methods. On the north coast, near **Reqqa Point**, people harvest sea salt from the salt pans as their ancestors have done for centuries.

Gozo's capital, **Victoria**, lies roughly in the centre of the island and a visit to its historic citadel is a must. The hilltop towns of **Nadur**, **Xaghra** (pronounced 'Shah-ruh') and **Zebbug**, with their prominent church domes, are known as 'the three hills' and they are the island's original settlements. The fishing villages of **Marsalforn** and **Xlendi** (pronounced 'Shlen-di'), set around attractive bays, have developed as the main resorts for tourists.

Diving and swimming are excellent in the clear blue waters around Gozo's coastline. There are also good walks, both along the coast and inland. Although the island is small – only 64 sq km (25 sq miles) – there are enough places of interest to keep you busy for a fortnight. However, Gozo is not meant for rushing around, but for relaxing on its idyllic bays, sipping a coffee or a beer at its local bars and cafés, or enjoying a meal at its pleasant restaurants.

The ferry crossing from Cirkewwa on Malta to Mgarr on Gozo takes about 25 minutes. In high season the morning ferry gets very busy, so get there early.

BEACHES

Dahlet Qorrot Set around a little harbour backed by colourful fishermen's huts, the small, sandy beach of Dahlet Qorrot is popular with local families. There is also a very good coastal walk from here to Qala Point.

Hondoq ir-Rummien This pleasant, sandy beach below the village of Qala faces the island of Comino. It is good for children but can get very crowded at weekends.

Ramla Bay This wide stretch of soft reddish sand is Gozo's best beach, but, thankfully, it remains surprisingly uncrowded. Approach it on the road from Marsalforn. Above the beach is the fabled Calypso's Cave, now reduced by erosion to a mere cleft in the rock, but still a vantage point for a picture-postcard view.

San Blas This is the best little sandy cove on Gozo. It's quite a trek getting down to it and an even longer one climbing back up, but if you're fit and child-free, the good swimming here makes the effort well worthwhile.

THINGS TO SEE & DO

Azure Window

Eroded limestone has never been so spectacular as at Gozo's aptly named Azure Window at Dwejra Bay. Behind it, reached by a tunnel, is the saltwater lake known as the Inland Sea. If you can watch the sunset from here it will be a highlight of your holiday. Nearby is the offshore outcrop known as Fungus Rock, so-called because of a spongy plant, *fungus melitensis*, that grew there. It was used to cure stomach pains and to stem the flow of blood from injuries, and was so prized by the Knights that they built Qawra Tower opposite to guard the supply.

◓ *Victoria Square, Xaghra, with its parish church*

Calypso's Cave

According to legend this is where the nymph Calypso kept Odysseus
a 'prisoner of love' for seven years. More practically, it is a spot high on
the cliffs from where you get a stunning view of the shoreline and Ramla
Bay, famous for its beach of red sand. The viewpoint is easily reached by
road and there is a winding footpath down to the beach.

Diving

Gozo has several exciting all-year dive sites, including the renowned
Blue Hole at Dwejra Bay, on the western edge of the island, Coral Cave,
the Inland Sea and the Xlendi Bay Tunnel. Gozo is noted for dramatic
underwater rock formations, caves and tunnels. There is also a popular
wreck-dive site with the remains of a former ferry and two other boats

scuttled in the same locality. Most of Gozo's dive sites are easily reached from the shore and there are dive centres with PADI-qualified staff in all of the resorts who can arrange accommodation for a diving holiday on the island.

Altantis Diving Centre is in Marsalforn and offers PADI-certified courses and excursions. ⓐ Qolla Street, Marsalforn ❶ 2155 4685 ⓦ www.atlantis gozo.com ⓔ diving@atlantisgozo.com

◓ *Gozo's ancient temple of Ggantija*

Blue Waters Dive Cove ⓐ Kuncizzjoni Street, Qala ⓣ 2156 5626
ⓦ www.divebluewaters.com ⓔ info@divebluewaters.com
Calypso Diving Centre ⓐ Hotel Calypso, Marsalforn Bay seafront
ⓣ 2156 1757 ⓦ www.calypsodivers.com ⓔ info@calypsodivers.com
Frankie's Gozo Dive Centre offers beginners' dives, PADI courses and
diving holidays on their motorised sailing yacht. ⓐ Mgaar Road, Xewkija
ⓣ 2155 1315 ⓦ www.gozodiving.com ⓔ frankie@gozodiving.com
Moby Dives ⓐ Xlendi Bay ⓣ 2156 4429 ⓦ www.mobydivesgozo.com
St Andrew's Divers Cove is a fully equipped and PADI-certified dive
centre open all year and catering to first-timers as well as divers looking
for certification. ⓐ St Simon Street, Xlendi Bay ⓣ 2155 1301
ⓦ www.gozodive.com ⓔ standrew@gozodive.com

Ggantija

Along with Malta's other ancient temples, these 5,000-year-old remains
are the Earth's oldest free-standing structures, pre-dating even the
pyramids and Stonehenge. ⓐ Located on the outskirts of Xaghra
ⓣ 2155 3194 ⓛ 09.00–16.30 daily ⓘ Admission charge

Gharb Folklore Museum

All kinds of interesting commercial and domestic bygones are displayed
in a beautifully restored 18th-century house. Definitely worth a visit.
ⓐ 99 Church Square, Gharb ⓛ 09.30–16.00 Mon–Sat, 09.30–12.00 Sun
ⓘ Admission charge

Gozo Pride Tours

Full-day tours of Gozo by jeep or quad bike, or in combination with a
motorboat trip. Package includes pick-up from hotel, ferry to Gozo and
lunch. ⓣ 2156 4776 ⓦ www.gozopridetours.com

Marsalforn

Gozo's largest resort sits in a wide bay with its colourful fleet of
traditional *luzzus* sheltered in a tiny harbour next to the small
sandy beach. There are good waterfront restaurants and bars, a

promenade, watersports and bicycle hire. The salt pans along the shore to the west of the village date from the 18th century and are well worth a look.

Victoria

The island's tiny capital, with a population of just 6,400, was named in honour of Queen Victoria's diamond jubilee in 1897 (although locals still use the old name, Rabat). Independence Square is a charming and attractive spot with trim shady trees, old-fashioned shops, a handful of cafés and a morning market. Just off the square, the 17th-century Church of St George is known as 'the Golden Basilica' on account of its richly gilded Baroque interior. The medieval lanes behind the square are fun to explore.

The walled citadel perched above the streets of Victoria dates back to Roman times and was fortified by the Knights of St John in the early 17th century. The panoramic views over the island from the ramparts are stupendous. Behind its rather plain façade, the cathedral is a Baroque gem with a most unusual feature: when funds ran out before completion of the planned dome, the Italian artist Antonio Manuele painted a *trompe-l'oeil* dome. It was probably the only parish church on Gozo for several centuries.

Housed within the citadel precincts are several small museums, the best of which is the **Folklore Museum**, but there's also the **Cathedral Museum** (☏ 2155 6087 🕓 09.45–1630 Mon–Sat, closed Sun), the **Old Prison**, **Natural Science Museum** and **Museum of Archaeology**. Contact **Heritage Malta** (☏ 2155 3194 🌐 www.heritagemalta.org 🕓 09.00–16.30 daily) for information on these museums.

TAKING A BREAK

Bellusa Café £ Small friendly café in an old town house near the fish market. The tables outside are ideal for people-watching in Victoria's main square. ⓐ 34 Independence Square, Victoria ☏ 2155 6243 🕓 07.00–19.00 daily

Brookies Pub & Restaurant ££ Family-run restaurant beneath the walls of the citadel. The fish is very good. Pasta and local dishes are also on the menu. ❷ 1–2 Wied Sara Street, Victoria, on the main road to Zebbug ❶ 2155 9524 ❺ 18.30–23.30 Wed–Mon, closed Tues

Otters Bistro ££ Stylish modern eatery on the water's edge with a terrific view of Marsalforn Bay. Excellent salads, pasta and fish, and a great wine selection. ❷ Saint Mary Road, Marsalforn ❶ 2156 2473 ❺ 12.00–17.00, 19.00–24.00 Mon–Sat, 12.00–24.00 Sun

AFTER DARK

RESTAURANTS

Ta'Rikardu (Riccardo's) £ Cosy family-owned restaurant in the narrow lanes of the citadel in Victoria, close to the cathedral. The fresh home-made vegetable soup is fabulous and never the same from one day to the next. Gozitan salad of peppered goat's cheese, sun-dried tomatoes, onion, capers and olives is a speciality. Also unusual is rabbit cooked in Riccardo's home-produced wine. A small shop sells Gozitan produce, honey, liqueurs and hand-crafted glass. ❷ 4 Fosos Il Street, Cittadella, Victoria ❶ 2155 5953 ❺ 09.00–18.00 Mon–Sat, 09.00–16.00 Sun

Xerri Il-Bukkett £ Gorgeous views over Mgarr Harbour to neighbouring Comino and Malta are to be had from the terrace of this hilltop bar and restaurant. Rabbit, fish and home-made ravioli are among the specialities. The local *bocci* (a game like *boules*) club is adjacent to the bar. ❷ Zewwieqa Road, Qala ❶ 2155 3500 ❺ 11.30–15.00, 17.30–22.00 Mon–Fri, 11.30–22.00 Sat & Sun

L'Ankra ££ You can watch the boats coming and going from the big windows of this restaurant overlooking Mgarr Harbour. Fresh fish, pasta and local specialities. ❷ 11 Shore Street, Mgarr ❶ 2155 5656 ❺ 18.00–22.30 Mon–Sat, 11.30–14.30 Sun

Auberge Chez Amand ££ This delightful bistro and restaurant, with a cool terrace overlooking the beach, serves delicious Maltese specialities and Mediterranean dishes, such as *gbejniet* (cheese) salad, seafood *amandine* and cannelloni thermidor. A friendly spot run by Belgian chef Amand and his daughter Caroline. ❸ Qbajjar Road, Marsalforn ❶ 2156 1188 ❸ Lunch and dinner Thur–Tues, closed Wed

Huan Yuan ££ Highly rated Cantonese restaurant on the hill leading up from Mgarr Harbour, next to L'Ankra. ❸ Shore Street, Mgarr ❶ 2156 5700 ❸ 18.30–22.30 daily; also 12.00–14.30 Sun (winter)

Il-Kartell ££ Set in three adjacent former boathouses by the harbour in Marsalforn, with a summer terrace on the water's edge. Varied menu of Mediterranean and Maltese dishes, including plain grilled fresh fish and *qara baghli mimli* – marrow stuffed with minced pork, beef and cheese.

SHOPPING

Handmade lace is a Gozitan speciality and highly prized for its quality. Best deals are in the craft shops at **Ta'Dbiegi Crafts Village**, located in a former army barracks in St Lawrenz. Rosanna's, located at Shop 2, has a vast array of lace, hand-knitted woollens, shawls, tablecloths and other items at very reasonable prices. **Pins & Needles** produces handcrafted leather items on-site, including passport covers, purses, key fobs and belts. **Ta'Dbiegi Jewellery** in Workshop 1 is a small workshop where you can see a range of gold and silver items being made.

Look for **Gbejniet**, Gozo's tasty sheep's-milk cheese, which you can buy as small peppery rounds in jars from the market in Victoria, or from shops.

Arkadia is Victoria's shopping mall in Fortunato Mizzi Street, and has some interesting boutiques. **Junction 66** has high-quality gifts, fine glassware, china figurines and wooden clocks.

📍 Marina Street, Marsalforn ☎ 2155 6918 🕐 11.30–15.30, 18.00–22.30 Thur–Tues, closed Wed

Salvina ££ A beautifully restored rustic house serving excellent island dishes. Specialities are rabbit, pan-fried or in a stew, local poultry and fish. 📍 21 Frenc ta'l-Gharb Street, Gharb ☎ 2155 2505 🕐 11.00–15.00, 18.00–22.00 daily

Stone Crab ££ Some of the best fish on Gozo can be had at this waterside restaurant, as well as pizzas and pasta. Carnivores can tuck into an excellent steak rossini. 📍 Marina Street, Xlendi Bay ☎ 2155 6400 🌐 www.thestonecrab.com 🕐 11.00–23.00 Fri–Wed, closed Thur

NIGHTLIFE

La Grotta is a popular club in the countryside near the fishing village of Xlendi. It's partly in a cave with an open-air dance floor. 📍 Xlendi Road, Xlendi (about 2 km/1 mile from Victoria) 🕐 24.00–dawn (summer)

Victoria has two opera houses, the **Aurora** and the **Astra**, built by rival philharmonic societies and both still going strong. When there is no opera, the theatres are used as cinemas.

🔺 *Xlendi, one of Gozo's main tourist resorts*

⬥ *Comino's fabulous Blue Lagoon*

Comino

Midway between Malta and Gozo, and covering just 2.5 sq km (1 sq mile), Comino is the smallest of Malta's inhabited islands. It takes its name from the herb, cumin, which grew wild here in former times. Once a pirate haven, the island is now home to an away-from-it-all hotel specialising in watersports, plus a handful of farmers who somehow eke a living from this barren, sun-baked rock. There are no roads and no cars. Some tours allow you to explore the island, though there is little to see, apart from the hotel, an ancient chapel and the **Santa Marija Watchtower** (which doubled as the Chateau d'If in the 2002 movie *The Count of Monte Cristo*), built by the Knights in the early 17th century. Surprisingly, this tiny spot has a police station, and Mass is held once a week in the old chapel.

Comino's great attraction is the **Blue Lagoon**. Its heavenly turquoise waters above a seabed of soft white sand are fantastic for swimming and snorkelling, and the underwater caves and grottoes are perfect for scuba divers. However, the tiny cove can become very crowded with day-trippers and cruise-boat passengers. If you want to swim, make sure you stick to the lagoon, as there are jellyfish in the harbour and their stings can be quite painful. On the opposite shore is the uninhabited rock islet of Cominotto.

Most people visit Comino as part of a day cruise from Malta or Gozo. In summer there are also small boats that ferry passengers on the 15-minute trip to the Blue Lagoon from Malta's Cirkewwa Harbour several times a day; from Gozo the ten-minute ferry trip operates on a regular basis. If you decide to explore Comino, take plenty of water, a hat and extra sunblock, as there is little shade. The hotel is closed in winter, so bring food and drink as well if you visit then.

Malta panorama

The centre of the island holds much of interest, and a day away from the resorts will do much to round out your experience of Malta. The easiest way to do this is to take a tourist coach tour. The itinerary can vary, but typically begins at one of Malta's most remarkable churches at Mosta, travels back in time to the island's original capital at Mdina, visits the Ta'Qali Craft Village for a bit of shopping, stops for lunch at a village restaurant and ends at the picture-postcard fishing village of Marsaxlokk.

THINGS TO SEE & DO

Limestone Heritage
An unusual tourist attraction giving an insight into Malta's traditional stoneworking, located in an old quarry from which the rich honey-coloured limestone was extracted. You can try chiselling a piece of limestone to make your own souvenir. ⓐ Mikiel Azzopardi Street, Siggiewi ⓣ 2146 4931 ⓦ www.limestoneheritage.com ⓔ info@limestoneheritage.com ⓛ 09.00–16.00 Mon–Fri, 09.00–12.00 Sat, closed Sun

Malta Sightseeing
Tours by hop-on, hop-off open-top bus, starting from Sliema. The Red Tour visits attractions in the southern half of the island, including the Valletta Waterfront, the Three Cities, the Tarxien Temples and Marsaxlokk. The Blue Tour visits the northern and western half, including Mosta, Ta'Qali Craft Village, Dingli Cliffs and Golden Bay. ⓐ Supreme Travel Ltd, Castellana Road, Zejtun ⓣ 2169 4967 ⓦ www.maltasightseeing.com ⓔ info@maltasightseeing.com ⓛ 09.00–15.00 daily; Blue Tour every hour, Red Tour every half-hour

Marsaxlokk
The name Marsaxlokk (pronounced 'Marsa-shlock') derives from *Marsa* (the Port) and *xlokk* (the sirocco wind). This is the most picturesque

fishing village on Malta and, despite the coachloads of visitors it receives daily, it has remained remarkably unspoilt. Its quayside is the perfect place for a cheap fish lunch and there is a daily market where you can haggle over lace tablecloths and other goods.

🔺 *Marsaxlokk's photogenic harbour*

THE EYES OF THE *LUZZU*

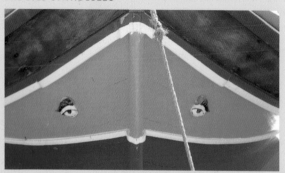

Few visitors leave Marsaxlokk without taking a picture of the traditional Maltese fishing boat, the *luzzu* (pronounced 'lut-sue'). Each *luzzu* is painted on either side of its unusually high prow with its own pair of eyes. This tradition goes back, along with the design of the *luzzu*, to Phoenician times (some 2,500 years ago) when the eye was first painted as a good-luck charm to ward off the dreaded Evil Eye. Ironically, often painted alongside this pagan charm is the name of a Catholic saint.

Mosta Dome (The Church of St Mary)

This church was built between 1833 and 1860. Its portico and triangular gable are based on the Pantheon in Rome, but more famous is its dome, which measures 40 m (131 ft) in internal diameter and has given the church its more familiar name. This is claimed to be the third-largest church dome in the world after St Peter's in Rome and St Sophia in Istanbul.

It is said that the dome was built so large not as an act of deliberate pomposity, but because St Mary's was literally built around an existing church, which could not be demolished until the new one was complete! The interior, trimmed with 18-carat gold leaf, is a marvellous sight. The floor is set with an unusual geometric pattern.

During the Blitz of 1942 it is said that at least two bombs bounced off the dome. A third bomb, however, dropped straight through while the church was full with some 300 parishioners. By good fortune, bad technology, or – as the Maltese say – the grace of God, it failed to explode, and so another island miracle was born. A replica of the bomb is displayed in a side room of the church. ⓐ Triq Il-Parrocca, Mosta

Palazzo Parisio

This 18th-century mansion has lavishly decorated ceilings and frescoes, antiques, paintings and bronzes. Its gardens are still impressive. ⓐ Victory Square, Naxxar ⓣ 2141 2461 ⓦ www.palazzo parisio.com ⓔ info@palazzoparisio.com ⓛ 09.00–18.00 Mon–Sat ⓘ Admission charge

Tarxien Temples & Hypogeum

Located in the midst of one of the town of Tarxien's suburbs, the Tarxien Temples (pronounced 'Tar-she-en') were built between 3800 and 2500 BC. Stonehenge is about the same age. This is Malta's largest temple complex, and three of its six temples have been partially reconstructed. The Central Temple is the most impressive and was the last to be built. There are many fascinating remains, including altars with animal reliefs, an enormous stone bowl used for ritual purposes, and stone balls thought to have been used to roll the huge slabs from which the temple is constructed into position.

Just 100 m (110 yds) away is Malta's most fascinating temple complex. The subterranean Hypogeum is a unique prehistoric monument in the town of Paola that was discovered accidentally by builders in 1902. Archaeologists found a complex underground system of passages and chambers with carefully crafted masonry arches and columns. The deepest section is 10 m (33 ft) below street level. Wall paintings in delicate red ochre still survive. The Hypogeum is now a UNESCO World Heritage Site. The number of visitors is strictly limited each day, so advance booking is essential. ⓣ 2169 5578 ⓛ 09.00–16.30 daily

◓ *The Blue Lagoon and view of Comino*

Mediterranean cruise

Located far from the polluting influence of mainland Europe, the blue waters around Malta are some of the clearest and cleanest in the Mediterranean. You cannot say you have truly seen the Maltese archipelago unless you have explored its coastline from the seaboard side at least once. Here is a taste of the tours on offer – check with the tourist office for further details.

THINGS TO SEE & DO

The Blue Lagoon

Not to be confused with the Blue Grotto (see page 86), the glorious waters that divide the island of Comino from the islet of Cominotto are the biggest draw in Maltese cruising. Shallow and sheltered, the waters are not only a lovely inviting colour, but they are warm as well. Some trips make this their sole destination for an entire day – great if you just want to spend the whole time lazing around, but with very little in the way of coastal sightseeing to offer. This idyllic place can become very crowded, which means your boat may anchor a little way out, leaving you a long swim before you can put your feet down – check before you book. The Blue Lagoon is also the perfect location for scuba diving, and there are several diving schools operating in the area that run organised trips.

Grand Harbour Tour

The defence system that protects Valletta and the Three Cities is without any question one of the world's great feats of military architecture. The achievement is rendered still more remarkable by the fact that many of these bastions and fortifications were built over 400 years ago. The only way to gain a full appreciation of this amazing complex is from the water, on a tour of the Grand Harbour, with a commentary full of lively anecdotes. ⓐ Departs from Sliema ❶ Tours last 90 minutes

Harbour Air Seaplanes

This is without doubt the most spectacular way to see the islands. Viewed from above, Malta takes on a completely new dimension – often cluttered and untidy at ground level, the island seems neat and well ordered from the air, especially the grid-pattern streets of Valletta. Other highlights include the Grand Harbour, Mdina, Victoria (Gozo), Comino and the Blue Lagoon. There is a 30-minute tour of the islands and a shorter 10-minute trip to Gozo, landing at and taking off from Mgarr Harbour. The DH-3 De Havilland Single Otter seaplane takes off from Sliema Creek or the Grand Harbour in Valletta, and flies at 1,000 feet. Time in the air simply flies by, so the longer trip is recommended if you can afford it. ⓐ Upper Vault 2, Pinto Wharf, Valletta ⓣ 2212 8302/ 8309 ⓦ www.harbourairmalta.com

Hera Cruises

Tour company offering a choice of cruises:

The 'Round Malta 360°' Cruise Departing from Sliema, this tour takes you clockwise around the island, to the picturesque fishing village of Marsaxlokk (see page 78), and the less-than-picturesque industrial Malta Freeport. The tour continues past the famous Blue Grotto (see page 86), the dramatic Dingli Cliffs (see page 89), the sandy beaches of Golden Bay (see page 29) and the strange sight of Sweethaven Village (see page 35). A leisurely stop is made in the Blue Lagoon for a swim and the option of 'doing the Oki-Koki'. Lunch is served on-board, then it's back to Sliema via St Paul's Bay and the little islands where the Apostle was allegedly shipwrecked.

Sailing Cruise Most cruise boats are motorised. If you would prefer a more romantic voyage, try the *Fernandes* or the *Hera*, beautiful Turkish *gulets* (pronounced 'goo-let') or the fully rigged 70-year-old schooner *Charlotte Louise*. Combining old-fashioned sail and sleek modernity is the *Spirit of Malta* (summer only), bringing a touch of the Caribbean to the Mediterranean, with its lively music and unrationed

🔺 *There is a lot of good diving along the coast of Malta*

rum. Most cruises return by 18.00, but when the sun goes down the fun begins on the 'Fernandes Sunday Sunset Cruise' and the 'Spirit of Malta Party Night'. 🅐 4 Triq Abate Rigord, Ta'Xbiex 🕐 2133 0583 🅦 www.heracruises.com

Luzzu Cruises

Harbour cruises and trips from Sliema to Marsaxlokk Bay on-board a traditional Maltese fishing boat. 🕐 7906 4489 🅦 www.officialluzzu cruises.com 🅔 luzzucruises@onvol.net

The Blue Grotto & the southwest

The southwest coast of the island is well known for its rugged rocky scenery. The Blue Grotto is Malta's most famous natural formation but the Dingli Cliffs are the most spectacular. Between these lie the island's most dramatically sited temples.

THINGS TO SEE & DO

Blue Grotto

The Blue Grotto is the biggest and best of a series of sea caves and archways near the village of Zurrieq (pronounced 'Zur-ree-ay'). Small boats pick up passengers in the sheltered picturesque rocky inlet of Wied-iz-Zurrieq and take them on a 25-minute tour. The eroded limestone grottoes and arches are awesome in scale, and the effect of sunlight on the water is magical. The water is brilliantly clear and in the caves it takes on a deep blue hue as the sunlight reflects off the rock and back into the water. Put your hand in the water and even that will look blue!

Buskett Gardens

Most of Malta's trees were cut down a long time ago by medieval shipbuilders, and Buskett Gardens is today the only reminder that this was once a wooded island. The term 'gardens' is, in fact, a bit of a misnomer, as most of this area consists simply of woodland. Not surprisingly, given its uniqueness, it is a popular place for picnics, and on 29 June (the feast of St Peter and St Paul – also known as *Mnarja*, pronounced 'Im-nar-yah'), thousands of people come here to celebrate.

The attractions of the area have also long been appreciated by Maltese rulers. On the edge of Buskett Gardens is Verdala Palace, built in 1586 as a summer residence for the Grand Master of the Knights of St John. Today it is the summer house of the president of Malta.

△ *Blue Grotto*

◔ The standing stones of Hagar Qim

Dingli Cliffs

Malta's highest point is 250 m (820 ft) above sea level, measured from the very edge of the Dingli Cliffs down the sheer rock face to the sea. Even on this, farmers have managed to cultivate some tiny terraces.

The cliffs run for virtually the entire southwestern coast of Malta. The normal sightseeing route is to drive to Rabat and then on to the village of Dingli; they are 1 km (½ mile) or so beyond the village.

Nearby is one of Malta's strangest mysteries. Cut into the flat rocky surface of the ground are long parallel grooves, rather like old tramlines. It is thought that these may have acted as runners for early forms of transport, and are often referred to as 'cart ruts'. The area near Dingli, where these are to be found in large numbers, is known colloquially as Clapham Junction.

Hagar Qim & Mnajdra

These two adjacent temple complexes are among the most impressive prehistoric monuments on Malta. Both are around 4,500 to 5,000 years old. The first site you will visit is Hagar Qim (pronounced 'Aa-jah eem'). Its name translates as 'standing stones', for very obvious reasons – one of its giant slabs alone measures 3 m by 7.5 m (10 ft by 25 ft). Hagar Qim is in better condition than its neighbour Mnajdra (pronounced 'Im-nah-ee-dra'), which was vandalised and seriously damaged a few years ago. Both were shrines to Mother Earth, and one school of thought is that worshippers believed that the dead would only return to her womb if sacrifices were made at these places. Certainly offerings of animals' blood and milk were made at both temples.

Mnajdra looks on to the smallest of the Maltese islands, **Filfla**, a tiny rock which may have had a ritual importance once upon a time, but has more recently been used for target practice by the Royal Navy. Today it is uninhabited and is protected as a bird reserve.

If you want a good place to cool off on this stretch of coast, you can't beat **Ghar Lapsi**, a superb natural lido, which is usually only frequented by locals. It is located around 6.5 km (4 miles) due west of Hagar Qim and Mnajdra.

Wine tourism

Malta has an ideal climate for growing grapes and there is a flourishing wine-production industry – though nowhere near the scale of Italy, France or Spain. Wine bars are a growth industry all over the islands and there is a demand for assured high-quality wine from Malta's own vineyards, spurred on by an increase in tariff-free imports of French and Italian wine since Malta joined the European Union. Maltese winemakers also produce wine from grapes imported from Italy.

Finding out about Malta's winemaking industry is an entertaining way of spending time away from the beach. Guided tours of wineries and cellars are available at some of the winemakers' premises and you can take part in tutored wine-tasting sessions. The vineyards make an attractive scene in some otherwise dull pieces of countryside.

Chardonnay, Syrah and Cabernet Franc are the most common grape varieties grown on Malta and Gozo, but there are also two varieties that are unique to the islands: the white Girgentina (which produces crisp dry white wine) and red Gellewza grapes (which produce fruity medium-bodied red and fine rosé wines). Harvesting takes place by hand in August, earlier than in other countries because the grapes ripen more quickly in Malta's hot and humid climate. To increase the growing of grapes and meet the demand for locally produced wine, the government has made grapevines a priority crop, and farmers can get subsidies if they work with winemakers and use their land for growing grapes.

Camilleri Winery

Camilleri is a small specialist producer of premium wines from grapes grown entirely on Malta, and holds wine tastings at its retail outlets.
ⓐ Master Wine Buildings, Oratory Street, Naxxar ⓣ 2549 2000
ⓦ www.camilleriwines.com ⓔ info@camilleriwines.com

Emanuel Delicata

Delicata is the largest producer of Maltese wine and the originator of an annual wine festival in Valletta at the beginning of August, and one on

⬥ *Delicata's vineyards stretch out below the town of Mdina*

Gozo in early September. Groups of over 20 people are welcome at Delicata's 17th-century cellars, which have tasting vaults and regular tutored tastings. Phone or email to enquire and make a reservation. ⓐ The Winery on the Waterfront, Paola ⓣ 2182 5199 ⓦ www.delicata.com ⓔ info@delicata.com

Marsovin

The best-known producer of Maltese wine is Marsovin, which has five vineyard estates, including one on Gozo. The Marsovin winery has cellars that were originally built around 1620 as workshops and stores for the docks in the Grand Harbour. Book a cellar tour by phone or through the Marsovin website. ⓐ The Winery, Wills Street, Marsa, Paola ⓣ 2182 4918 ⓦ www.marsovin.com ⓔ info@marsovin.com ⓘ Visits by appointment

Meridiana

The Ta'Qali Wine Estate was planted in 1994 and 1995 with Chardonnay, Cabernet Sauvignon, Merlot, Syrah and Petit Verdot grapevines. Meridiana's wine cellars are constructed in traditional local style, about 4 m (13 ft) below ground, to keep the wine cool. Try their unfiltered red wines, especially Melqart and Celsius, which are matured for 12 months in French oak barrels. ⓐ Meridiana Wine Estate, Ta'Qali ⓣ 2141 3550 ⓦ www.meridiana.com.mt ⓔ info@meridiana.com.mt ⓛ Cellar shop 09.00–16.00 Mon–Fri, 10.00–12.00 Sat, closed Sun ⓘ Tours & tastings by appointment

ⓞ *The island's buses are colourful period pieces*

LIFESTYLE
Island life

⬥ As on most islands, fish is always on the menu!

Food & drink

There are few establishments in the tourist resorts that serve exclusively Maltese cuisine. Many restaurants serve a handful of Maltese dishes but alongside these you will find a variety of international fare on the menu. Most restaurants on the island are Italian.

FOR STARTERS

Every Mediterranean country has a fish soup and Malta is no exception; here it is called *alijotta*. The most common soup is *minestra*, similar to Italian minestrone and made of a host of different vegetables. If you are a pasta fan, try the Italian-inspired *ravjul* (ravioli filled with cheese). A very typical Maltese cheese dish is *gbejniet* (or *gbejna*), a pungent round of peppered sheep's-milk cheese, usually served with salad.

SEAFOOD

This will vary by season and availability to a restaurant, but typical fish dishes might contain *acciola* (amberjack), *cerna* (grouper), *espadon*, *pixxispad* or *pesce espada* (all names for swordfish) and *lampuki* (dorado). The last is a Maltese speciality, and is in season from September to November. It is often served in a pie (*torta tal-lampuki*) mixed with tomatoes, onions, olives and various other vegetables. A much more robust-tasting speciality is Maltese-style swordfish, smothered in a tasty sauce of tomatoes and capers. Another enjoyable local seafood dish is octopus, often served in a dark tomato sauce. Other unusual fish names you may come across are *dott* (stone bass) and *dentici* (sea bream).

RABBIT

The islanders' favourite meat dish is *fenek* (rabbit). This may be served *biz-zalza* (casseroled) or fried. Rabbit is the Maltese celebration dish, and a traditional *fenkata* evening usually comprises a menu of spaghetti with rabbit sauce, followed first by roast rabbit, then by nuts and figs. As a special treat it may be served as a pie (*torta tal-fenek*) with pork, peas, tomatoes and other ingredients. You will have to use your fingers to get the bones out of the rabbit, but the dish is tasty and justifies the effort.

MORE MEAT DISHES

Aside from rabbit, the other classic Maltese meat dish is *bragioli*, made from a flattened beef fillet, stuffed with bacon, breadcrumbs and hard-boiled eggs, rolled up and simmered in wine with onions. Less common on restaurant menus are Maltese sausages, which are of the familiar British link variety (as opposed to the continental slicing style). Often flavoured with lemon and herbs, these are delicious.

CHEESE & PASTA

Two favourite national dishes which strongly reflect the Italian influence are *timpana* – baked macaroni with meat, eggs and cheese (and perhaps

⬥ *Olive oil – a staple ingredient in Mediterranean cooking*

peas and aubergines), topped with flaky pastry – and *ross-fil-forn* –
savoury rice, baked with eggs and meat. You may also find these sold
from street stalls in square containers as takeaway snacks.

SNACKS

Typical Maltese snacks are sold in cafés or street kiosks. The ubiquitous
lunchtime filler is *hobz biz zejt*, which translates as 'bread with oil'.
This is a delicious, typically Mediterranean, snack of bread smeared
with a paste of tomatoes, garlic, capers and olive oil, then filled
with tuna, olives and salad. It may also be served toasted (like
Italian bruschetta) as a starter in restaurants. Some places advertise
hobz biz zejt as 'Maltese bread'.

A favourite morning snack is a *pastizzi rikotta* (flaky ricotta-cheese
envelope) or *qassatat* (pronounced 'ass-er-tat'), a round flaky or
shortcrust pie, filled with either cheese or lightly spiced marrowfat peas.
The latter is sometimes referred to as a *pastizzi tal-pizelli*. Both are sold
fresh from the oven, and are best eaten warm.

SWEET THINGS

The Maltese have a sweet tooth and it is always a treat to pop into
a *pastizzerija* for a coffee, accompanied by a pastry or another of the
confections on offer. Nougat is very popular and nougat vendors are an
integral part of the village *festa*.

DRINKS

The Maltese have inherited coffee from the Italians and tea from the
British, but coffee is nearly always a better bet. The British have also
bequeathed to the Maltese a dark, cold, fizzy, pale ale, sold almost
everywhere under the Hopleaf brand. Cisk Lager (pronounced 'Chisk') is
its companion brew. Maltese wines have come on in leaps and bounds
in recent years, and the island's better-quality vintages can be excellent.
Gozo makes its own wines, which are gutsy and tend to have a higher-
than-average alcohol content. The national soft drink is Kinnie, a
refreshing fizzy drink, flavoured with bitter oranges and aromatic herbs.

Menu decoder

Most restaurants on Malta serve international food, but you may come across the following Maltese specialities in bakers' shops, street stalls or rural cafés.

alijotta Fish soup, not dissimilar to the classic French *bouillabaisse*, powerfully packed with garlic.

kabocci mimlija Cabbage leaves stuffed with minced beef or cheese, parboiled then shallow-fried.

bragioli A popular meat stew, made with bacon, eggs, wine and onions.

kanolli ta-rrikotta Croissants stuffed with ricotta cheese blended with chocolate, almonds and preserved cherries.

kappunata Similar to ratatouille, a vegetable stew made with aubergines, peppers, onions, tomatoes and courgettes, garlic and capers.

Kinnie A bitter but refreshing local drink made from bitter *chinotto* oranges and a variety of aromatic herbs and spices.

mqarets Deep-fried date pastries, which are part of the island's Arab legacy. Their tempting aroma wafts around Valletta's City Gate.

pastizzi Puff-pastry pasties stuffed with mashed peas and spices or ricotta cheese.

ravjul Ravioli with a difference – stuffed with locally made ricotta cheese.

timpana Another traditional pie, this time of Sicilian origin, made from minced beef, potatoes, eggs and pasta in a white sauce, and topped with puff pastry.

torta tal lampuki A traditional pie of Arabic origin (blending sweet and savoury ingredients), eaten as a summer snack. Different cooks have different recipes combining *lampuki* (also known as dorado – a meaty white fish similar to mackerel) with some or all of the following: spinach, puréed cauliflower, onions, garlic, tomatoes, chestnuts and sultanas.

○ *Alfresco dining on Valletta Waterfront*

Shopping

CRAFT VILLAGES

For the best range of Maltese handicrafts – lace, filigree jewellery, chunky woollen jumpers, woodwork, metalwork, glass and so on – try the **Ta'Qali Craft Village**, on Malta, where you can watch local artisans at work, or the smaller complex of **Ta'Dbiegi**, just outside St Lawrenz, on Gozo (see page 74).

GLASSWARE

Glass is perhaps the island's most striking product, often produced in beautiful hues of gold and blue. Maltese- and Gozitan-blown and handcrafted glass is not cheap but the quality is high and you can watch the pieces being made in open workshops. Leading makers are Mdina Glass and Valletta Glass at Ta'Qali Craft Village, Phoenician Glass on Manoel Island and Gozo Glass.

⬥ *There are many markets to wander around*

LACE

Lace is another speciality. Look out for tablecloths, napkins, shawls and handkerchiefs. Maltese lacemakers are a dying breed, and if you are not buying from a traditional outlet, where you can see artisans at work, watch out for imitations imported from the Far East.

MARKETS

The markets in Valletta are the best on the island. The Sunday-morning market, known as the Monti, just outside the City Gate, has an interesting flea market section but is mostly full of tourist fare and counterfeit products from the Far East. There is a lively bustle to the market, and it is worth a visit to see a slice of everyday Maltese life. The daily market on Triq Il-Merkanti (Merchants' Street) features much the same style of merchandise.

SILVER & GOLD

More portable than glass, and often just as beautiful, is the delicate filigree silver and gold jewellery produced by Maltese artisans. You can see them at work in many places and prices are often competitive.

VALLETTA

In the narrow streets of the capital city you will still find small shops that have survived virtually unchanged since the 1940s, alongside a growing range of modern high-street names and fashionable boutiques.

Valletta Waterfront is the in-place for shopping as well as socialising. Mdina Glass has a showroom in the converted vaults, a branch of Pedigree Toyshop selling a huge range of gifts and souvenirs has opened nearby, and you can choose a diamond or gold accessory at Sterling Jewellers. There's also an Agenda Bookshop, a Bristow Potteries outlet that stocks a large selection of Maltese handcrafted ceramics, and a branch of The Mics selling straw hats, caps, shoes and woodcraft gifts. Bijoux Terner sells stylish bags, hats, pashminas, belts and sunglasses.

Children

LWS ANIMAL PARK

Emus, deer, llama, monkeys, mountain goats and rabbits are free to run around the landscaped wilderness gardens, and a visit to the LWS Animal Park is both educational and an entertaining day out. The animals are well cared for and not confined to cages. A train winds its way around the park and gardens, and in the centre there is a pedal go-kart track. Horses and ponies are on hand for rides, and the park caters for people of limited mobility. ⓐ The Park of Friendship, Zinzell Street, Marsaskala ⓣ 2163 6526 ⓛ 09.00–13.00 Mon–Fri, 09.00–12.00 Sat (viewing only), 09.00–17.00 Sun ⓘ Admission charge (includes a train or go-kart ride for children on Sun)

MEDITERRANEO MARINE PARK

Next door to Splash & Fun Water Park (combined tickets are available for both, the entertainment here includes shows with sea lions, turtles, parrots and cockatoos. But the real stars are the dolphins, rescued from the Black Sea, who perform crowd-pleasing stunts. Moreover, adults and children over eight can have the thrill of a lifetime by getting wet and actually swimming with them. ⓣ 2137 2218 ⓦ www.mediterraneo park.com ⓛ 10.00–18.00 daily (15 June–15 Sept); 10.00–16.45 Tues–Sun, closed Mon (16 Sept–14 June) ⓘ Advance booking essential.

PLAYMOBIL FUNPARK

Look around the Playmobil factory and watch the toys being made. Outside, there are hours of fun to be had playing in a Playmobil park. ⓐ HF80, Industrial Estate, Hal Far ⓣ 2224 2445 ⓦ www.playmobil malta.com ⓛ 10.00–18.00 Mon–Sat, 10.00–13.00 Sun (July–Sept); 10.00–18.00 daily (Oct–June)

SPLASH & FUN WATER PARK

Water slides and tubes, jets, pipe falls, water guns, a wave pool – just about everything for fun in the water! Don't miss the Lazy River (ride an inflatable ring through cascading waterfalls) or the Space Bowl (a thrilling dark tube that sends you swirling around a large bowl before you drop into the pool below). ⓐ Located on the main coast road between St Julian's and St Paul's Bay at Bahar Ic-Caghaq (just ask the bus driver for Splash & Fun) ⓣ 2137 4283 ⓦ www.splashandfun.com.mt ⓔ info@splashandfun.com.mt ⓛ 09.30–18.00 daily (23 Apr–25 June & 12–25 Sept), 09.00–21.00 daily (26 June–11 Sept), closed 26 Sept–22 Apr

YOUNG TEENAGERS

Pack your children off to one of the special, alcohol-free, early-evening weekend discos in Paceville (at St Julian's), or make a family visit to the tenpin bowling alleys of **Eden SuperBowl** (see page 22). If the thought of Mdina, the Silent City, doesn't appeal, tell them about **Mdina Dungeon** – gruesome waxworks of actual medieval horrors (see page 60).

● *The fantastic slides at Splash & Fun Water Park*

Sports & activities

HORSE RIDING

The friendly, helpful Golden Bay riding centre (see page 34) is equally at home with experienced riders and complete novices. You can ride for one or two hours, following trails along the coastal paths and overlooking the beaches, amid some of the island's least-spoilt countryside.
ⓣ 2157 3360 **ⓘ** Book ahead

MARSA SPORTS CLUB

Right in the centre of the island, the Marsa Sports complex offers a wide range of activities. This includes the only golf course on Malta – the 18-hole Royal Malta Club (equipment is for hire) – 17 tennis courts, 5 squash courts, mini-golf, an open-air swimming pool and billiards.
ⓐ Aldo Moro Street, Marsa **ⓣ** 2123 3851 **ⓦ** www.marsasportsclub.com

⬥ *Mellieha is excellent for watersports*

TYPICALLY MALTESE

Horse racing, of the trotting variety, is the most popular spectator sport on Malta. Jockeys do not ride the horses but are pulled along behind on a flimsy-looking trap. The track is at Marsa (public buses and organised excursions run there) and meetings on winter Sundays pull in large crowds. Racing continues throughout most of the year. Enjoy a flutter on the tote or with the course bookies. The other Maltese sporting speciality is waterpolo. You can see top-quality league games staged in the 'pitches' on the seafront at several places (including Sliema, St Paul's Bay and St Julian's) on summer weekends. ● See local papers for details of fixtures

WALKING

March to June and October are the best months for walking on Malta and Gozo. The latter is particularly pleasant as there is more unspoilt countryside to ramble around Ask at the tourist office for a local guide to take you out, or, alternatively, do it yourself with the assistance of *Hiking in Malta, Gozo & Comino*, published by J. Kolb Publishing (mostly aimed at experienced walkers) and available at bookshops in Valletta, if not in your resort.

WATERSPORTS

The island's clear blue waters and warm summer seas, which average 23°C (73°F) mean that diving is a very popular pastime. The scarcity of sand, lack of pollution and stillness of the virtually tide-free waters all contribute to excellent visibility, which on average is up to 30 m (100 ft). You won't see too many exotic fish, but there are caves and grottoes to explore, and good wreck diving. Most clubs on the island operate to a high standard, are PADI and BSAC affiliated, and are well equipped to deal with beginners and experienced divers.

At Golden Bay, Mellieha Bay, and at various lidos around the island, you will find the usual range of resort watersports, including windsurfing (the conditions at Mellieha and Golden Bay are excellent), waterskiing and jet skis.

LIFESTYLE

Festivals & events

CARNIVAL

Held in the week before Lent (usually mid-February to early March), this is one of the most colourful events of the Maltese festival calendar. It culminates in a procession of floats featuring grotesque characters with giant heads. Open-air dancing competitions are also held. Festivities take place in various locations, though the main ones are in Valletta and, just outside, Floriana.

FESTA

The islands' most visual cultural celebration is the village *festa*, or festival. The purpose of the *festa* is to honour the patron saint of a particular village. Various events, mostly of a religious nature, are conducted from Wednesday through to Sunday. The religious highlight is the Sunday night procession, when a weighty statue of the saint is carried shoulder high by sturdy villagers.

The whole village will be festooned with banners, with the church as the centrepiece, gloriously decorated with hundreds of coloured lights outside and with sumptuous red damask inside. Some of the other buildings, such as the village band clubhouse, will be similarly lavishly decorated.

The village brass band, and possibly visiting brass bands, parade and play, and, on Saturday night, singers may join in to perform an outdoor concert in the village square.

Traditional Maltese nougat is sold from gleaming, portable wood-and-glass cabinets, and there are fast-food vendors too. Saturday night climaxes with a marvellous display of powerful fireworks set in place on large wooden stands dotted around the village centre. Aerial fireworks are saved until the sun sets, and they bring the *festa* to a spectacular finale.

The *festa* season on Malta begins in mid-April and lasts until September, with at least one festival being celebrated somewhere on the island each week.

🔺 Festa *night*

⬤ *A religious procession*

THE PERFORMING ARTS

For an evening of conventional high culture, visit Valletta's **Manoel Theatre** (see page 42). This little gem stages regular productions of ballet, opera, concerts and plays. Look in the local paper to see what's on.

The **Isle of MTV** concert (Ⓦ www.isleofmtv.com) is the highlight of Malta Music Week, held in June. The concert sits alongside an assortment of wild club nights and beach parties.

Other annual highlights are the **Malta Jazz Festival** in July, and the **Malta Arts Festival** (Ⓦ www.visitmalta.com), which runs over from July into August. During the Arts Festival opera singers perform in front of historic monuments and in Mdina's main square with the cathedral as a backdrop.

▶ *Traditional horse-drawn carriage transport in Valletta*

PRACTICAL INFORMATION
Tips & advice

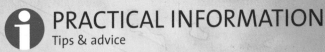

Accommodation

Malta has a vast range of hotels and apartments. Prices are very competitive, but of course the best deals are found outside the high season. The hotels below are graded by approximate price:

£ budget   **££** mid-range   **£££** expensive

BUGIBBA & QAWRA

Coastline Hotel ££ Large resort hotel overlooking Salina Bay, near Bugibba and St Paul's Bay. The health and leisure centre has a gymnasium, sauna, heated jet pool and treatment room. **ⓐ** Salina Bay **ⓣ** 2157 3781 **Ⓦ** www.coastline.com.mt **ⓔ** info@coastline.com.mt

San Antonio ££ Large hotel complex with extensive grounds, including a pool and sun terraces fringed with palm trees. Excellent fitness and spa facilities and a choice of restaurants. **ⓐ** Qawra **ⓣ** 2158 3434 **Ⓦ** www.sanantonio-malta.com **ⓔ** info@sanantonio-malta.com

Suncrest Hotel ££ Large hotel on the promenade with its own lido, the Sun and Surf beach club, accessed by a tunnel under the road. Good dining, with the first-class restaurant, It-Tokk, serving Mediterranean and Maltese dishes; also home to a pizzeria, Tal-Kaptan. **ⓐ** Qawra Coast Road, Qawra **ⓣ** 2157 7101 **Ⓦ** www.suncresthotel.com **ⓔ** reservations@suncresthotel.com

COMINO

Comino Hotel & Bungalows ££ The only accommodation on the island of Comino. The hotel overlooks San Niklaw Bay and the bungalows are in Santa Marija Bay with their own private swimming beach. **ⓣ** 2152 9821 **Ⓦ** www.cominohotel.com **ⓔ** info@cominohotel.com

GOLDEN BAY

Radisson Blu Golden Sands Resort & Spa £££ Brand new family-friendly hotel and spa resort built on the cliffs overlooking Golden Bay with sea-view rooms. Three splendid restaurants, including Agliolio on the beach. ☎ 2356 1000 🌐 www.radissonblu.com

MDINA

Xara Palace £££ The only hotel within the town of Mdina. Upmarket and elegant, in a restored 17th-century building set within Mdina's medieval walls. Ask for one of the rooms on the upper floors, which offer stunning views over the island. There are two restaurants: De Mondion for fine dining and Trattoria AD 1530. ⓐ Il-Kunsill Square ☎ 2145 0560 🌐 www.xarapalace.com.mt

MELLIEHA

Solana ££ Value-for-money hotel in a low-rise limestone building, with its own swimming pool and a rooftop hydro-massage pool. Some rooms have a view over to Gozo and Comino and the ferry is close by. ⓐ Gorg Borg Olivier Street ☎ 2152 2209 🌐 www.solanahotel.com.mt ✉ info@solanahotel.com.mt

ST JULIAN'S & PACEVILLE

Bay Street Hotel ££ A large hotel (it has 100 en-suite rooms) close to the action in lively Paceville. The hotel reception is reached through the Bay Street Complex. A buffet breakfast is served in the All Seasons Restaurant on the fourth floor. Rooftop swimming pool on the seventh floor. ⓐ St George's Bay ☎ 2138 4421 🌐 www.baystreet.com.mt

Cavalieri Hotel £££ This four-star hotel is on the water's edge in St Julian's, on the doorstep of the Portomaso Marina, and close to most of the resort's attractions. ⓐ Spinola Road ☎ 2318 0000 🌐 www.cavalierihotelmalta.com

ST PAUL'S BAY

San Pawl Hotel £ Good-value family hotel in a quiet residential area within a few minutes' walk of the old village of St Paul's Bay and the resorts of Bugibba and Qawra. Outdoor and indoor pools.

ⓐ Blacktail Street ⓣ 2157 1369/1370 ⓦ www.sanpawlhotel.com
ⓔ info@sanpawlhotel.com

Ambassador ££ Good-value modern hotel on the water's edge on the Xemxija side of St Paul's Bay. Large seawater pool and Internet café.
ⓐ Shipwreck Promenade, Xemxija ⓣ 2157 3870 ⓦ www.ambassador
malta.com ⓔ info@ambassadormalta.com

Gillieru Harbour Hotel ££ Small family-run hotel on the water's edge with views over the bay to St Paul's islands. Very convenient for shops and the promenade. ⓐ Church Square ⓣ 2157 2720
ⓦ www.gillieru.com ⓔ gillieru@maltanet.net

SLIEMA
Europa £ This well-located, value-for-money hotel on the seafront in central Sliema is run by a friendly young team. The cool Mojito Bar serves excellent cocktails. ⓐ 138 Tower Road ⓣ 2133 4070 ⓦ www.europa
hotelmalta.com

Bayview Hotel ££ Refurbished and upgraded hotel and self-catering-apartment complex on the Sliema seafront, overlooking the Marsamxett Harbour and the Valletta skyline. ⓐ 143 The Strand, Gzira-Sliema ⓣ 2132
0216 ⓦ www.bayviewmalta.com ⓔ info@bayviewmalta.com

Hotel Fortina £££ This four-star hotel is handily situated near the ferry stop for Valletta, and has a top-class thalassotherapy facility, the Spa Mediterranée, which offers treatments using seawater and seaweed.
ⓐ Tigné Seafront ⓣ 2346 2346 ⓦ www.hotelfortina.com

VALLETTA
British Hotel ££ One of Malta's oldest family hotels; located in the capital city of Valletta, with a great view from the dining room over Grand Harbour. ⓐ 40 Battery Street ⓣ 2122 4730/2123 9022
ⓦ www.britishhotel.com ⓔ info@britishhotel.com

Preparing to go

GETTING THERE

The cheapest way to enjoy a stay on Malta is usually to book a package holiday with one of the leading tour operators, such as Thomas Cook. The flight time from Britain to Malta is just over three hours. **Air Malta** (W www.airmalta.com) operates twice-daily flights from Heathrow, up to nine flights a week from Gatwick, five a week from Manchester and two a week from Birmingham. It also flies from some smaller regional airports, including Exeter and Cardiff, during the summer. **easyJet** (W www.easyjet.com) has a year-round service to Malta from Gatwick, Manchester, Liverpool and Newcastle; it also operates direct flights from Belfast. **Ryanair** (W www.ryanair.com) operates weekly flights from Dublin, Luton, Bournemouth, Leeds-Bradford, Birmingham, Edinburgh and Bristol direct to Malta. **Bmibaby** (W www.bmibaby.com) flies year-round to Malta from East Midlands Airport. Charter flights from Gatwick and various regional airports such as Bristol and Leeds-Bradford are available from Thomas Cook, **Thomson Airways** (W www.thomsonfly.com), **First Choice** (W www.firstchoice.co.uk) and other leading tour operators, usually as part of an inclusive tour. All these operators have partnerships with hotels and can provide good-value package deals year-round. Charter flights are also a good choice for off-peak flight-only bargains if you already have somewhere to stay on Malta or Gozo.

If you know when you can travel it pays to book your flight well in advance to get the best prices. If your travelling times are flexible, and if you can avoid the school holidays, you can sometimes find cheap last-minute deals using the websites of the leading holiday companies. **Malta International Airport** ☎ 2124 9600 W www.maltairport.com

MALTA TOURIST OFFICE

Further information about Malta can be obtained from the **Malta Tourist Office**. ⓐ Unit C Park House, 14 Northfields, London SW18 1DD ☎ 020 8877 6990 W www.visitmalta.com

The Malta Tourism Authority has information offices at:

Malta International Airport @ Arrivals Lounge 🕿 2369 6073/6074
🕔 10.00–21.00 daily

Valletta @ 229 Auberge d'Italie, Merchants Street 🕿 2291 5440
🕔 09.00–17.00 Mon–Sat, 09.00–12.30 Sun

Victoria (Gozo) @ Tigrija Palazz, Republic Street 🕿 2156 1419
🕔 09.00–12.30, 13.00–17.00 Mon–Sat, 09.00–12.30 Sun

DOCUMENTS

The most important documents you will need are your tickets and your passport. Check well in advance that your passport is up to date and has at least three months left to run (six months is even better).

All children, including newborn babies, need their own passport now, unless they are already included on the passport of the person they are travelling with.

It generally takes at least a week to process a passport renewal. This can be longer in the run-up to summer. For the latest information on how to renew your passport and processing times check with the **Identity and Passport Service** on 🕿 0300 222 0000 or 🌐 www.ips.gov.uk

You should check the details of your travel tickets well before your departure, ensuring that the timings and dates are correct.

If you are thinking of hiring a car while you are away, you will need to have your driving licence with you. If you want more than one driver for the car, the other drivers must have their licences too.

MONEY

Malta is a member state of the European Union and the euro is the national currency. All major credit cards are acceptable in Malta for shopping and paying hotel bills, except in the smallest establishments. Cash machines (ATMs) are plentiful in the main towns so you can take money out using a debit card, Visa, MasterCard, Cirrus or Link card.

Traveller's cheques have rather fallen out of favour since credit cards became the main method of paying bills, and you will need to go to a main bank branch or to a Thomas Cook office to exchange them.

INSURANCE

Have you got sufficient cover for your holiday? Check that your policy covers you for loss of possessions and valuables, for activities you might want to try – such as scuba diving, horse riding, or watersports – and for emergency medical or dental treatment, and flights home if required.

CLIMATE

The hot months are from June to September when the average daytime temperature is around 32°C (90°F) and there is little rain. Sea breezes bring welcome relief, but Malta is also subject to the hot humid *xlokk* or sirocco winds that blow from the Sahara Desert. October is still warm and sunny but rainfall is frequent. The winter months can be cold and wet, but are still mild compared to northern Europe. Springtime is warm and sunny and can be the best time to visit Malta.

AIRPORT PARKING & ACCOMMODATION

If you intend to leave your car in an airport car park while you are away, or stay the night at an airport hotel before or after your flight, you should book well ahead to take advantage of hotel discounts and cheap off-airport parking. Airport accommodation gets booked up several weeks in advance, especially during the height of the holiday season. Check whether the hotel offers free parking for the duration of the holiday.

PACKING TIPS

Baggage allowances vary according to the airline, destination and the class of travel, but 20 kg (44 lb) per person is the norm for luggage that is carried in the hold (it usually tells you what the weight limit is on your ticket). You are also allowed one item of cabin baggage weighing no more than 5 kg (11 lb), and measuring 46 by 30 by 23 cm (18 by 12 by 9 in). A handbag counts as one item.

In addition, you can carry your airport purchases as hand baggage. Large items (surfboards, golf clubs, collapsible wheelchairs and pushchairs) are usually charged as extras – let the airline know in advance if you want to bring these.

CHECK-IN, PASSPORT CONTROL & CUSTOMS

Allow yourself plenty of time for airport security checks, which can be lengthy, especially in the busy summer months. All metal objects, electronic devices such as MP3 players and laptop computers, and coats and jackets must be placed in trays for scanning in the X-ray machines. You may also be required to take off your shoes and put them through the scanner as an additional random security check.

Liquids and gels such as suntan lotion and toothpaste that you want to take in your carry-on bag must be in containers no larger than 100 ml and placed in a clear plastic bag for inspection. Larger liquid items must be in your checked-in luggage or they will be confiscated.

You are restricted to just one item of carry-on baggage, which must be small enough to fit into the overhead storage bins in the aircraft cabin. A handbag counts as one item, so if you want to take another bag through, you should place the handbag inside it.

There are no customs restrictions on alcohol and tobacco when travelling between Malta and other countries of the EU, but you should be aware that there is no duty-free allowance either. Prohibited items include firearms, pornography, meat, poultry and their by-products, plants and recreational drugs.

Entry or transit visas are not required for stays of up to three months for holidays or unpaid business trips by nationals of most Commonwealth countries, UK dependencies or European Union members. If a stay of longer than three months is planned, applications should be made in person, before the end of the initial three-month period, to the Principal Immigration Officer, Immigration Police, Police Headquarters, Floriana.

Nationals of countries that require a visa should obtain these from a Maltese embassy or consulate. Where neither of these is available, a written request should be made to the Commissioner of Police, Police Headquarters, Floriana – faxed applications are acceptable. 🕿 2124 7777 Application forms can also be downloaded from 🌐 www.foreign.gov.mt

Visitors requiring an entry visa to Malta and who undertake day trips (of less than 24 hours) to another country are exempted from paying another entry visa on their return to Malta.

During your stay

AIRPORTS

Malta International Airport is located next to the village of Gudja, 10 km (6 miles) from Valletta.

Land-side facilities at MIA include airline ticketing offices and aviation counters, baby-care rooms, two banks, cafeterias, car-hire offices, a chapel, pharmacist, flight information counter, florist, international telephone, lotto booth, newsagent, post office, restaurant, sweets shop, telecommunications centre, tourist information counter and a viewing gallery.

Air-side facilities include baby-care facilities, bar/cafeteria, duty-free shops – in both arrivals and departure halls – and three VIP/executive lounges (the Ewropa Lounge is operated by Air Malta, while the La Valette Executive and Gerolamo Cassar (arrivals hall) lounges are run by the airport operating company – Malta International Airport plc.

BEACHES

The coastlines of the Maltese islands are on the whole rocky and not renowned for their sandy beaches. The rock generally slopes down very gently for a long way into the sea.

There are several sandy beaches in the north of Malta; the best are Mellieha Bay, Gnejna Bay, Golden Bay, Ghajn Tuffieha and Paradise Bay. In the south, the finest is Pretty Bay in Birzebbuga, and, Gozo, Ramla Bay stands out for its red sand. Comino has two sandy beaches – Santa Marija Bay and St Nicklaw Bay. Rock bathing is possible at almost all

BEACH SAFETY
A flag system operates, to advise you of swimming conditions.
Red = dangerous – no swimming at all
Yellow = strong swimmers only – exercise caution
Green = safe bathing conditions for all

other beach sites. In many areas the rocks are flat and worn smooth and can be very slippery. You should also take care about rocks under the water, which can be jagged and cause a nasty gash if you fall.

An alternative to beach swimming is to use lidos, enclosed pools with decks and sunbeds, usually operated by hotels but open to the general public. Some have access to a private stretch of open-sea beach.

Malta is striving to have all beaches classified under the EU's Blue Flag system, which is a sign that the beach is safe. A Blue Flag beach will have a lifeguard patrol during the daytime, but many beaches still do not have lifeguards.

CASINOS

There are four casinos on Malta: the **Dragonara Casino** in St Julian's, the **Casino di Venezia** in Vittoriosa the **Oracle Casino** at the Dolmen Resort Hotel in Qawra and **The Casino** at Portomaso, the new marina complex in St Julian's. You need to produce identity (a passport will do) for admittance. Foreign nationals must be over 18 and Maltese citizens 25, and there is requirement for smart casual dress – for men this usually means a shirt and tie.

Maltese casinos have high-jackpot slot machines and the full range of table games, including roulette, blackjack and various styles of poker. They also have bars, high-class dining in sumptuous surroundings and musical entertainment. The Dragonara and Oracle also have courtesy bus services to and from the hotels in the St Julian's and Sliema areas.

ELECTRICITY

The electrical supply is 240 volts. The 13-amp, British-style three-pin rectangular sockets are used in Malta.

FACILITIES FOR VISITORS WITH DISABILITIES

Most hotels and visitor attractions now offer facilities for those with disabilities. Entrances and corridors are generally step-free and usually one lift has doors wide enough to take a wheelchair. Public places such as churches and historic sites have ramps, except where this is

> **EMERGENCIES**
> Staff manning the emergency services all speak perfect English.
> **On Malta** Police 🛈 191; Ambulance 🛈 196; Fire 🛈 199
> **On Gozo** Police and fire 🛈 2156 2044; Ambulance 🛈 2156 0600

impossible. If you require assistance at the airport, notify your airline at the time of booking and arrangements will be made for your arrival. See 🌐 www.knpd.org for further information.

GETTING AROUND

Bus

The Maltese bus service is cheap, efficient and a bit of an adventure. The buses themselves are very old, and on Gozo you can ride the classic British Leyland Super Comet from the 1950s, which is still in service. Many of the buses are driver-owned and are cleaned and looked after with tender loving care. They all show a route number, but you should check with the driver to be certain where the bus is going as they don't necessarily show the correct destination. You can't always rely on timetables, but most routes run every 20 minutes.

The main bus station for Valletta is immediately outside the main city gate. Sliema waterfront is also an important terminus and there is a bus station in Bugibba/Qawra. Buses to and from Cirkewwa are timed to meet the Gozo ferry, as are the buses at Mgarr Harbour for the drive to Victoria.

A new shuttle-bus service runs direct from the international airport to Cirkewwa (for the Gozo ferry) and is an economical and efficient alternative to taxis. The journey takes about 40 minutes.

Car hire

Renting cars in Malta is generally cheap. A national driving licence is sufficient. The main international car-hire firms such as Hertz and Avis are represented at the international airport and in the main resorts. Your hotel reception can advise on renting cars from local companies, whose vehicles are cheaper but not as new. Petrol stations are open only in the daytime and it can be difficult to fill up on Sundays.

Car crime is not a major problem in Malta. The main danger is theft of possessions from parked cars. Attendants will often look after your car at beaches and archaeological sites. It is customary to give them a small tip (around 10 to 25 cents).

Driving As in many Commonwealth countries, driving in Malta is on the left. There is a speed limit of 80 km/h (50 mph) on highways and 50 km/h (30 mph) in urban areas. Third-party insurance is advisable, as the island's accident rate is one of the highest in Europe. International and national driving licences are acceptable and may be endorsed for free at the police headquarters in Floriana (☏ 2122 4001/9).

In the event of an accident, telephone the police on 191 and, if required, an ambulance on 196. If the collision is severe, drivers should not move cars until the police have arrived and taken note of the incident. Insurance companies will not entertain any claim unless it is supported by a police report. In the event of minor accidents, a form – obtained from any police station – must be completed.

Taxi

It is a common irritation for visitors that Maltese taxi drivers don't always start their meters at the beginning of a journey, so you don't really know how much the trip is going to cost unless you agree it before getting into the car. Taxis are not cheap, so overcharging should not be tolerated. Taxi fares are governed by law, but the law is rarely enforced unless customers complain to the **Malta Transport Authority** (☏ freephone 8007 2393).

Hotel reception staff can call a taxi or a private hire car (usually black) and get the price at the time of booking. Taxis are essential if you go out at night, as the bus services stop at 22.00, apart from a few night buses running from Paceville to the main resorts to cater for the nightclub crowd.

Fares from the international airport are more strictly enforced and you would normally pay in advance at a booth in the Arrivals terminal, and hand a voucher to the taxi driver. Fares from the airport (and the sea passenger terminal) are set. As an indication, expect to pay around €15 from the airport to Valletta, €20 to St Julian's, €25 to St Paul's Bay or Golden Bay, and €32 to Cirkewwa for the Gozo ferry (exact fares are subject to annual review). Airport fixed rates apply at all times including at night, Sundays and public holidays.

HEALTH MATTERS

There are no particular health hazards in Malta excepting the risk of sunburn. Tap water is safe to drink but may taste strange to foreigners; bottled water is easy to find in shops and cafés.

No inoculations are required, though a yellow fever certificate is needed if you have been in an infected area.

Malta offers free basic health care to EU citizens on production of a European Health Insurance Card (EHIC). This is not a substitute for medical cover on travel insurance and would not cover the costs of a hospital stay or repatriation after a serious illness or accident. Nor does the EHIC entitle you to free ongoing or non-urgent medical treatment; it simply entitles the holder to the level of free medical treatment that locals get. You can apply for an EHIC free of charge online at Ⓦ www.ehic.org.uk, by calling the UK Department of Health (🕿 0845 606 2030) or by filling in a form from any post office. Malta also has reciprocal health agreements with Australia.

If you are undergoing medical treatment at the time of your visit to Malta, stock up on enough medicine or tablets before you leave.

There are two state-run hospitals on Malta: St Luke's in Guadamagia and Mater Dei in Birkirkara; and one on Gozo, Gozo General Hospital in Victoria. If you need an ambulance in an emergency, dial 196 on Malta or 2156 0600 on Gozo.

There are dentists in most towns, and all speak English.

INTERNET

Most resorts and hotels have Internet access points and new Internet cafés are opening all the time. Charges for Internet time vary, but expect to pay about €1 per hour.

MEDIA

There are two locally published English-language daily newspapers – the *Malta Independent* (Ⓦ www.independent.com.mt) and *The Times of Malta* (Ⓦ www.timesofmalta.com) – and both have Sunday editions, along with the bi-weekly *Malta Today* (Ⓦ www.maltatoday.com.mt). English newspapers are also available from newsagents, usually in the late afternoon on the day of publication. A free English-language listings guide, *Events Malta*, is published monthly and is packed with information.

USEFUL WEBSITES

About Malta Ⓦ www.aboutmalta.com
Air Malta Ⓦ www.airmalta.com
Gozo Ⓦ www.gozo.com
Malta International Airport Ⓦ www.maltairport.com
Malta Tourism Authority Ⓦ www.visitmalta.com
Malta Weather Ⓦ www.maltaweather.com

OPENING HOURS
Banks
These are generally open 08.30–14.00 Monday–Thursday and until 15.30 on Friday. Many banks now open on Saturday mornings until 12.00. There are ATMs (cash machines) in most towns. You can exchange traveller's cheques at the main branch of a bank.

Bars, cafés & restaurants
Most bars close at 01.00, but in St Julian's and Paceville many also act as nightclubs and have longer hours. Restaurants tend to open at around 11.30 for lunch but then close in the afternoon and reopen for dinner service at around 19.00.

Chemists
These open during normal shopping hours, and have a rota system for Sunday mornings: 09.00–12.30 on Malta and 07.30–11.00 on Gozo.

Post offices

Standard post office opening hours are 07.45–13.30 Monday–Friday, and 09.00–12.00 on Saturday. The main post office at Qormi (a 305 Qormi Road) and the Gozo post office (a 129 Republic Street, Victoria) have longer opening hours, 08.15–16.30 Monday–Friday, 08.15–12.30 Saturday. Stamps can be bought at hotel receptions.

Shops

Traditional shop opening hours are 09.00–13.00 and 16.00–19.00, but many shops in resorts stay open all afternoon and some until 22.00. In villages, local shopkeepers adhere to the siesta tradition. Most shops close on Sundays and public holidays, except those geared towards souvenirs and holiday shopping.

PUBLIC HOLIDAYS

These can be great fun if you are looking for a party with the locals, but be aware that many shops and historic sites are closed on public holidays.

1 Jan	New Year's Day
10 Feb	Commemoration of St Paul's Shipwreck
19 Mar	Feast of St Joseph
31 Mar	Freedom Day
Mar/Apr	Good Friday and Easter (dates vary)
1 May	Labour Day
7 June	*Sette Giugno*
29 June	St Peter and St Paul (*L-Imnarja*)
15 Aug	Assumption of Our Lady (Santa Marija)
8 Sept	Victory Day, Birthday of the Virgin Mary
21 Sept	Independence Day
8 Dec	Immaculate Conception
13 Dec	Republic Day
25 Dec	Christmas Day

RELIGION

The majority of Maltese are Roman Catholic. There are small Anglican, Church of Scotland, Greek Catholic and Orthodox, Jewish and Muslim communities.

TELEPHONES

Maltese local telephone numbers are generally eight digits, beginning 21 for land lines and either 79 or 99 for mobiles. For calls into Malta, the country code is 356. To get hold of an international operator dial 1152, and for local directory enquiries dial 1182.

Malta is fully integrated into the mobile phone roaming network, so you should be able to use your own mobile phone for calling and receiving calls, albeit at a price.

Most coin-operated public phone boxes can be used only for local calls, but red British-style public phone boxes now accept cards and some are also email-enabled. International phone calls can also be made from Internet cafés. You can buy a local pay-as-you-go SIM card at the GO Mobile customer service desk in the arrivals hall at Malta International Airport.

TELEPHONING MALTA

To call Malta from the UK, dial 00 356 then the eight-digit number – there's no need to wait for a dialling tone.

TELEPHONING ABROAD

To call an overseas number from Malta, dial 00 followed by the country code (UK = 44), then the area code (minus the initial 0) and then the number you want.

TIME DIFFERENCES

Malta is on Central European Time (CET), one hour ahead of GMT (Universal Time) in winter and two hours ahead from the last Sunday in March until the last Sunday in October. Malta is six hours ahead of Eastern Standard Time (EST), seven in the summertime.

ACKNOWLEDGEMENTS

Thomas Cook Publishing wishes to thank the photographers, picture libraries and other organisations, to whom the copyright belongs, for the photographs in this book.

David Browne (pages 28, 41, 55, 57, 75, 93, 99, 103); Dreamstime/Drimi (pages 37, 65); Dreamstime/Mccarthystudio (page 96); Emanuel Delicata (page 91); Thomas Cook Tour Operations (pages 5, 9, 13, 18, 22, 33, 44, 69, 79, 82, 85, 87, 100, 104, 107, 108); Richard Williams (pages 10–11, 70, 80, 109); World Pictures (pages 26, 76, 88, 94).

For CAMBRIDGE PUBLISHING MANAGEMENT LIMITED:
Project editor: Ed Robinson
Layout: Paul Queripel
Proofreaders: Tom Lee & Kate Taylor
Indexer: Marie Lorimer

Send your thoughts to
books@thomascook.com

- Found a beach bar, peaceful stretch of sand or must-see sight that we don't feature?

- Like to tip us off about any information that needs a little updating?

- Want to tell us what you love about this handy, little guidebook and, more importantly, how we can make it even handier?

Then here's your chance to tell all! Send us ideas, discoveries and recommendations today and then look out for your valuable input in the next edition of this title.

Email to the above address or write to:
pocket guides Series Editor, Thomas Cook Publishing, PO Box 227, Unit 9, Coningsby Road, Peterborough PE3 8SB, UK.

Useful phrases

English	Maltese	Approx pronunciation
BASICS		
Yes	Iva	*eeva*
No	Le	*lay*
Please	Jekk joghgbok	*yek keeoshbok*
Thank you	Grazzi	*gratsee*
Hello	Bongu	*bonjou*
Goodbye	Sahha	*sah-ha*
Excuse me	Scuzani	*scoozanee*
Sorry	Scuzani	*scoozanee*
That's okay	Mhux problema	*moosh problema*
I don't understand	Mhux qed nifhmek	*moosh et nifmek*
Do you speak English?	Titkellem bl-Ingliz?	*titkellem blee ingliz*
Good morning	Bongu	*bonjou*
Good afternoon	Wara nofs in-nar it-tajjeb	*wara nofsinar it tie-eb*
Good evening	Bonswa	*bonswa*
Goodnight	Il-lejl it-tajjeb	*eel-layl it tie-eb*
My name is ...	Jisimni	*yi-simni*
NUMBERS		
One	Wiehed	*wea-het*
Two	Tnejn	*tneyn*
Three	Tlieta	*tlea-ta*
Four	Erbgha	*er-ba*
Five	Hamsa	*ham-sa*
Six	Sitta	*sit-ta*
Seven	Sebgha	*se-ba*
Eight	Tmienja	*tmean-ya*
Nine	Disgha	*di-sa*
Ten	Ghaxra	*ash-ra*
Twenty	Ghoxrin	*oshrin*
Fifty	Hamsin	*hamsin*
One hundred	Mija	*mi-ya*
SIGNS & NOTICES		
Airport	Ajruport	*ayruport*
Bus station	Terminus tax-xarabank	*terminus tash sharabank*
Smoking/non-smoking	Tista' tpejjep/Tpejpux	*tista tpeyyep/tpeypoosh*
Toilets	Toilets	*toilets*
Ladies/Gentlemen	Nisa/Irgiel	*neesa/eerjeel*
Subway	Sabwej	*sab-wey*